WORKERS, FACTORIES, AND
SOCIAL CHANGE IN INDIA

Workers, Factories, and Social Change in India

BY RICHARD D. LAMBERT

PRINCETON, NEW JERSEY

PRINCETON UNIVERSITY PRESS

1963

Publication of this book
has been aided by the Ford Foundation program
to support publication, through university presses,
of works in the humanities and social sciences

Richard D. Lambert is Professor of Sociology,
University of Pennsylvania

Printed in the United States of America
by Princeton University Press
Princeton, New Jersey

FOREWORD

▯▮▯ THIS IS THE FIFTH publication embodying results of the Gokhale Institute's investigation into some aspects of socio-economic life in Poona City. The publication thus reflects the continuing bias of field projects at the Institute towards the immediate environment. However, in many other ways the publication is unusual. It presents results of the work of a visiting foreign scholar who carried out by himself, and very intensively, a project of deliberately limited coverage. The project was directed chiefly towards collection of empirical data in relation to important propositions accepted currently in the literature on industrialism and labour commitment.

Most theoretical or descriptive socio-economic work in connection with underdeveloped countries embodies a common view regarding the situation in these countries. This is that the varying situations represent stages in the progress from tribalism, feudalism, traditionalism, etc., to modernity. By modernity is usually meant the existing situation in American and West European societies, which are supposed to be the ultimate goals, or at least necessary transitional destinations, of all these tribal, semi-feudal, and traditional societies. There are a number of ways in which the starting point, and the end destinations, are defined and described. Whatever the differences in basic assumptions and given points of departure, a fairly rigid predetermined path of progress is usually implied by most writers. Dr. Lambert has no elaborate construct of his own in this regard. He notes certain accepted formulations of the situation of factory workers in underdeveloped countries and of the stages in their progressive evolution, and uses them as the back-

v

ground against which to present the results of his intensive investigation into the situation in five Poona factories.

Dr. Lambert finds that in a number of ways his portrayal of the situation appears to differ from the results to be expected according to the accepted path of industrialism and its related phenomena. In this case it is obviously possible to argue that Dr. Lambert's choice of Poona, which is even today not highly industrialized, and which until some 20 years ago had grown only gradually, affording considerable scope for the migrant population to make adjustment in easy stages, affects his results. The picture of workers, their conditions of living and work, would not be expected to be the same in such a city as in one in which growth had been continuous and rapid and which was already highly industrialized. However, to put forward such a plea in relation to the validity of Dr. Lambert's comparisons is itself to raise important issues relating to generalizations about paths of development.

To my mind, the results of Dr. Lambert's investigations have interest in a number of other ways also. For example, they appear to indicate that where the industrial population is not dominant, grows slowly, and has time to adjust itself to its surroundings, factory groups mould themselves to the prevailing social pattern. Another aspect of this process of gradual adjustment is the manner in which the number of dependents in a family adjusts to the progress in income levels. The relative lack of mobility within groups of workers may also exhibit the force of traditional social pressures. At the same time, this study throws light on the situation regarding the market for labour.

In this connection, Dr. Lambert's attempt to evaluate the relative importance of caste and education in workers' progress has special importance. Though the findings in this case are not unequivocal, it is possible to argue on their basis that education and not caste is the more important determinant. If this is held to be true, it might well be claimed that the spread of general educational facilities throughout the country might prove to be the most important dynamic force in the existing situation. Educational attainments not only act as steps in the ladder of possible economic betterment within the urban economy, but also, in the larger context, they could have the result of converting, at least a part, of the increasing underemployment in rural areas into overt urban unemployment. The political and social pressures generated by such a movement could have a very strong effect.

Thus, apart from the phenomenon of compartmentalization of the market for labour, there is the fact of a chronic excess of supply to which attention has to be paid. The main result of the latter exhibited in Dr. Lambert's report is the average worker's quest for security. The importance attached to a secure though fixed position, the dominance of "influence" through caste and acquaintance ties, the prevailing attitude of fatalism among workers, brought out by Dr. Lambert, could as much be related to the pressures of the current situation relating to employment as to the value systems of traditional society.

Similar alternative interpretations could be offered relating to a number of parallels that Dr. Lambert draws between aspects of the situation of factory workers in Poona and traditional social institutions and beliefs. Notable among these is his finding that the worker looks upon his job as a piece of property and his comment that this could be compared to attitudes flowing from the "jajmani" system (known in Maharashtra as the "baluta" system), or his description of the total worker situation as a pigeonhole structure, which could well serve as a brief description of Hindu caste society.

It is part of the interest as well as of the insecurity of socio-economic formulations that alternative interpretations can, in most cases, be offered fairly readily. However, whatever the view one takes of particular aspects of Dr. Lambert's comments or findings, there is little doubt that this is a thorough piece of sound scholarship. It is a pleasure to record that he spared no trouble to attain an understanding of the inwardness of a complex and to him a strange situation. He has been at pains to set out his results in meticulous detail and to subject them to careful statistical analysis. I consider his discussion of the difficulties and of the methodology of investigations into workers' attitudes, such as that of favourableness to the company, of special value.

Gokhale Institute of
Politics and Economics
Poona, India.   D. R. GADGIL
November 20, 1962.

ACKNOWLEDGEMENTS

FINANCIAL SUPPORT for this research was provided by the John Simon Guggenheim Memorial Foundation, a Fulbright award, and the University of Pennsylvania's South Asia Regional Studies Department through a Faculty and a Summer Research Grant. Assisting in the collection of data were some twenty college students in Poona whose skill and dedication to the task were truly remarkable. I wish to commend especially Sri C. S. Natu who supervised the interviewing and coding. Without him, the project would have been severely crippled. I also wish to thank the Gokhale Institute of Politics and Economics, particularly Professors D. R. Gadgil, N. V. Sovani, V. M. Dandekar, and P. N. Mathur who acted as kind hosts, counsellors and patient listeners. I wish to thank also the workers, union officials, company owners, plant managers, and labor officers, all of whom were more than generous in giving their time and cooperation to the study. I am grateful to Professors N. V. Sovani, Morris D. Morris, Gladys Palmer, Phillip Sagi, and Marvin Bressler for having read and commented on the manuscript. A part of Chapter II was published in the *Journal of Asian Studies;* parts of Chapter V were printed in *Artha Vijnan* of Poona and the *Economic Weekly* of Bombay. — R. D. L.

CONTENTS

CONTENTS

WORKERS, FACTORIES, AND

SOCIAL CHANGE IN INDIA

CHAPTER I · INTRODUCTION

◼⁞◼⁞◼ THIS BOOK is aimed at two audiences: an audience interested in the substantive details of studies in industrial sociology or India, or both, and an audience interested in the general process of industrialization and economic development. Since the spheres of interest and tastes of the two audiences only partially overlap, it is hoped that patience will be displayed toward what must often seem like lengthy irrelevancies from one or the other viewpoint.

For the former group, this is a study of the workers in the five privately-owned factories in Poona, India. It reports on their demographic characteristics—age, sex, education, literacy, caste, family characteristics and migration history —both in comparison with the local non-factory population and in relation to each worker's position within the factory. It analyzes the previous occupational histories of the workers, the means by which they secured their current jobs, and their perceptions of the labor market. The nature of and criteria for hierarchical positioning in each factory, the degree of fit between wage and skill hierarchies, the history of horizontal and vertical mobility among the workers, the aspiration levels of various types of workers, job satisfaction and its relationship to hierarchical position, are all discussed. In view of the scarcity of empirical data on factory workforces in underdeveloped areas, the statistical results are presented in greater detail than they might ordinarily be. However, the techniques of statistical analysis used are relatively crude because of the uncertain error component of data drawn from a questionnaire study in a non-Western setting.

For the second of the two audiences, this study is con-

3

cerned with three different theoretical domains: one, problems in the recruitment and commitment of an industrial labor force in an agrarian society; two, factory typologies; and three, the factory as a social innovation.

RECRUITMENT AND COMMITMENT

How does this study differ from other work concerned with recruitment and commitment? There is a growing body of literature,[1] in part speculative, in part based upon anthropological field research, which views the recruitment of a committed industrial labor force as a strenuous and difficult process, both preceded and followed by a considerable amount of social and personal disorganization. The traditional way of life is seen as essentially resistant to the intrusion of industrialization, or, if not resistant, lacking in the cultural and social organizational overhead which supports the factory system in the West. The former thesis lies behind, for example, Slotkin's proposition that the available supply of factory labor is a function of the inability of the traditional society to meet the goals of its members. The number and social character of those available for factory employment depend upon the "cultural inadequacy" of the traditional society, and the groups in the society for whom it is least "adequate" are most available for factory labor.[2]

Many writers go beyond the question of the aggregate availability of workers and specify for each worker a de-

[1] The literature on this subject is ably summarized and synthesized by J. S. Slotkin, *From Field to Factory*, Glencoe, Ill.: Free Press, 1960; and by Wilbert E. Moore and Arnold S. Feldman in their introductory section to the symposium, which they edited, *Labor Commitment and Social Change in Developing Societies*, New York: Social Science Research Council, 1960.

[2] Slotkin, *op.cit.*, Ch. III and VI.

gree of "commitment" to his role in the industrial process. The most limited and probably original meaning of this omnibus term is reflected in one phrase of Charles Myers' book on Indian labor: "We can say that a 'committed' industrial labor force has developed when workers no longer look on their industrial employment as temporary."[3] In the full sentence of which this is a part, there are then appended several expandable phrases[4] which could lead to such a definition as the full one given by Kerr and Siegel: "It involves the setting and enforcing of rules concerned with the recruitment of a labor force, with the training of that labor force in the myriad skills required by the advanced division of labor, with the locating of workers in some appropriate pattern of geographical, industrial and occupational dispersion. It involves the setting of rules on times to work and not to work, on method and amount of pay, on movement into and out of work and from one position to another. It involves rules pertaining to the maintenance of continuity in the work process . . . the attempted minimization of individual and organized revolt, the provision of view of the world, of ideological orientations, of beliefs, the introduction of some checks on the individual insecurity inherent in an industrial order."[5]

Such a use of the term commitment leads, in turn, to the almost infinitely expanded one used by Moore and Feldman: "Commitment involves both performance and

[3] Charles Myers, *Labor Problems in the Industrialization of India*, Cambridge, Mass.: Harvard University Press, 1958, p. 36.

[4] For my general comments on the expandability of the concept of commitment, see Richard D. Lambert, "Labor in India," *Economic Development and Cultural Change*, 8:206-13 (Jan. 1960).

[5] Clark Kerr and S. Siegel, "The Structuring of the Labor Force in Industrial Society: New Dimensions and New Questions," *Industrial and Labor Relations Review*, No. 2, pp. 151-168.

acceptance of the behaviors appropriate to an industrial way of life."[6]

The data of this study, while they do not cover many of the categories enumerated by Kerr and Siegel, do not bear out the general thesis that what might be called the "recruitment-commitment problem" is so great a hindrance to industrialization as the literature suggests.[7] The factory workforce is not selective in Slotkin's sense, but represents a fair cross-section of the nearby population and, at least insofar as the worker's conviction that his employment is to be permanent is concerned, there is little evidence of either reluctance or ambivalence in his commitment.

The lack of support for the classic recruitment-commitment thesis in our data may possibly be a result of the difference in the setting of the factories here studied and the social environment in which many previous studies were conducted. The latter tended to be concerned with the most extreme situation: the most rural elements of the population are caught up in large extractive industries or in factories where repetitive machine operations contrast most strongly with their former work habits. Such studies have frequently confounded the effects of rapid, slum-producing urbanization with the factory situation itself, have dealt with relatively new factories that have not yet had time to become imbedded in the local institutional framework, or they have selected situations in which the locale surrounding the factory was either exclusively or predominantly agricultural. In such settings the contrasts

[6] Wilbert E. Moore and Arnold S. Feldman, *Labor Commitment and Social Change in Developing Areas*, p. 1.

[7] An argument, mainly on historical grounds, for the irrelevancy of much of the recruitment-commitment literature may be found in Morris D. Morris, "The Labor Market in India" in Moore and Feldman, *op.cit.*, pp. 173-200.

between the factory and non-factory workers are greatest, the culture shock strongest, the distaste of the neophyte worker for his new life presumably the most powerful, and the problems of maintaining a stable, highly productive labor force most difficult.

In the present study we are concerned with a different setting and a different stage of industrialization than the ones upon which most of the current recruitment and commitment theory has been based. In one sense it is inappropriate to compare our data with the expectations of a body of theory developed in situations closer to the agrarian end of the continuum. On the other hand, it is of interest to see the extent to which the anticipated problems of recruitment and commitment do operate in the setting we have chosen, since I would maintain that the present study describes a setting more typical of the context in which factories tend to be established in most under-developed countries. Most typically, the factories are in urban, not rural areas, and most towns and cities which serve as the setting for factories are characterized by the predominance of the tertiary sector (largely service) occupations rather than secondary sector (largely manu-facture) occupations. That is to say, a few factories are appended to centers already existing for other reasons, usually commerce or administration. Within these towns and cities, the factory labor force is drawn in large part from populations whose urbanization preceded their entrance into the factory system by many years, rather than from among peasants just off the land. Moreover, a large number of these factories might be called "mature," that is, stable in labor force and product over a number of decades.

The locale chosen for the present study illustrates this

situation fairly well. Poona, about 120 miles south of Bombay, is primarily an administrative and cultural center rather than an industrial city. Although about one-third of the earners in Poona in 1954[8] were employed in "manufacturing industries," this classification includes *bidi* making, repairing and servicing of motor vehicles, brass and copper works, and other small enterprises that lie outside the sphere of modern factory organization. While Poona's population doubled between the censuses of 1941 and 1951, from 278,165 to 480,982, its economy has been relatively constant over the past few decades. It is neither a metropolis itself, nor a satellite town. Factories have been part of the town life for many years, but they are not the dominant feature of the town's social and economic structure.

In this setting, the data show the inappropriateness of reading into the social analysis of the factory workforce the notion that it is peasant in origin and orientation, or at least that it is any more so than the general population. By and large, the workers already represent an industrial proletariat, and thus the enhancement of commitment has meaning only in the sense of their commitment to the company's goals—productivity and tractability—not tying them to a job. The data also raise the question of whether the concept of commitment should also be used for management as well as the worker, and we will conclude that the concept of reciprocal property rights in the job is a more useful way of viewing the situation than is commitment.

[8] One practical advantage of the selection of Poona was the fact that a cross-sectional survey of the social characteristics of the population, giving occupational and other economic data, had just been conducted in 1954. See N. V. Sovani, D. P. Apte and R. G. Pendse, *Poona: A Resurvey*, Gokhale Institute of Politics and Economics (Pub. No. 34), 1956, pp. 275, hereinafter referred to as Sovani, et al.

The proper question to ask is which aspects of the job the worker and the management, respectively, seek to control.

FACTORY TYPOLOGIES

When we speak at the broadest level of generalization, we often refer to the impact of industrialization as if it were a unitary process, identical in the organizational form that is being introduced if not in the consequences. At this quasi-metaphorical level, particularly when we consider the introduction of "the factory" into a non-industrial society as a sort of shock to established patterns, there is much to commend this usage. It permits attention to be focussed on cultural features in the indigenous society which may clash with, encourage, or are disrupted by this particular agent of social change. It is clear to all, however, that such a monolithic concept must crumble into many separate fragments once specific factories are studied in specific cultural settings. It will come as a surprise to no one that factories do differ, and yet there are very few attempts to classify factories in a way that will reflect either their differential recruitment and "impact" pattern or the internal organization of their work forces. It is, of course, impossible to develop a comprehensive taxonomic classification system based upon a sample of five factories in a single small city in India. On the other hand, certain characteristics of these factories do seem to reflect stable differences in structural features that would tend to appear frequently in developing economies, differences that would have important consequences for the career of the individual worker as well as the role of the factory in the larger society. These differences reflect sequential historical stages in the process of industrialization in the West, and are therefore presumably directly related to the character

9

and nature of the recruitment-commitment problems and "impact." The key elements in the typology are in the nature of the relationship between the worker and the machine, his fellow workers, and his supervisor.

As an agrarian society begins to mechanize, the first multi-worker units outside agriculture tend to be those engaged in the simple processing of raw materials. This predominance is especially marked when under colonial rule the more complicated manufacturing processes were, as in the case of India and Great Britain, performed in the metropolitan country. In colonies, to the extent that machinery is introduced, it is usually machinery into which the raw materials are fed and given their first-stage processing. In these as well as the mineral extractive industries, manpower can be organized into gangs, each with its own supervisor. Where machines are involved, one gang is assigned to the care and feeding of each machine. The characteristics of this form of organization are that there are many more men than there are machines, the machinery operates semi-automatically, and the workers' tasks are to insure that the machines consume and process materials somewhere near their maximal capacity. In such factories, workers possessing skills make up a relatively small proportion of the workforce. Those skills that are recognized are usually supervisory, or they may involve machine maintenance or adjustment, or the ability to work on the more complicated machinery. In our sample, three of the five factories were organized in this fashion, which we shall call Type A. One such factory, an older factory operating since the turn of the century, produces paper. Its manufacturing process is simple. Waste paper is mixed with rags manually, carried by head load (usually by women) and dumped into vats which reduce it to pulp. It is then fed through machinery which processes it, rolls it into paper, and cuts it to size. At the end of the process the sheets are counted manually, wrapped, and bound into reams. There is some ground for suspicion that the rate of production is geared to the speed of the count, rather than vice versa. Almost the entire product of the mill is bought by the Government of Bombay, and the mill has been under little pressure to rationalize its methods. Its labor force of 603 workers and its style of organization have remained largely unchanged over many years. The mill is absentee-owned. Its business affairs are managed by a professional managing agency firm, and the production process is supervised by a resident plant manager. It is not part of an industrial complex of mutually supporting or duplicating units. In style, it reminds one of a rural sugar or oil mill, that is, a one- or two-stage processing of raw materials by a few simple machines that are fed and tended by gangs of workers. The paper mill does, in fact, lie on the agricultural fringe of Poona, in Mundhwa, and many of its workers live in the villages surrounding the plant.

The same type of gang machine-tending and simple processing of raw materials also characterizes the chocolate and biscuit factory. It is, however, smaller, with only 159 employees, and more modern in both physical plant and technology. The chocolate and biscuit factory is family-owned and largely family-managed. It began in the owner's home in 1921 and has grown steadily since. The founder's sons have now acquired the technical training and education necessary to conduct the business and are engaged with him in the day-to-day operation of the factory. In 1952, the production process was rationalized and the factory was moved from the heart of the city to a new site out towards the growing industrial complex stretching up the main railway line toward Bombay.

Also of Type A is a rubber factory with 531 employees. Its production process involves relatively simple processing of raw materials by workers tending machines in gangs. Much of the equipment was imported from the West, and in its natural setting was mainly automatic and formed a continuous process. In the Poona factory the machinery is surrounded by large quantities of unskilled, manual workers. The factory began by producing balloons and now produces varied products from gum boots to hose. It is also family-owned and managed.

The second type of production system (Type B), which rose historically about the same time as the gang-organized factory in India, nevertheless represents a later stage in technological development. In such a factory, each worker tends one or more machines, performing operations which are almost entirely repetitive. Workers are no longer engaged in cooperative gang labor, but are individual operators clustered on the factory floor by the type of machine they tend and the nature of the machine's product. The skill of most of the workers is gauged by the rate at which they can make their machines produce, a skill which requires some minimal experience but which quickly reaches its peak and levels off. Such work is most easily rewarded by a piece-rate system of wages. In such factories, most workers are at the semi-skilled level. Their work is serviced by workers of less skill who man the power plant, bring in the supplies, carry away the finished product, sweep the compound, and so on. There is also a higher level of skilled workers similar in function to those found in the raw materials processing factories—repairmen, machine setters and adjusters, supervisors and coordinators—as well as those who have special skills on the more complex machines.

The largest factory in our study—the cotton textile mill with 2,342 workers at the time of the study—represents Type B. It has been in operation since the turn of the century, and is the lone survivor of several mills that once operated in the area. The factory premises, lying in the center of the city, are in the classic, turn-of-the-century mill style, with a high wall, busy compound, centrally located boiler room, long, humid sheds, tall tower, and a residential style headquarters with a veranda. In its organizational form and style of production, it is a carbon copy of the older mills in the Bombay complex of which it is really an isolated offshoot. Like the paper mill, it is absentee-owned and run by a managing agency and resident plant manager.

In the third style of organization (Type C), except for the supplementary service occupations, each worker not only feeds but individually directs a machine. His skill is absolutely necessary to the creation of the finished product; it is not spent solely to pace the operation of the machine. Such a production process normally requires many separate stages and the functions of the various work divisions within the factory need to be constantly interlocked. A gradually decreasing number of workers fills each higher skill category. The skilled workers are not different in kind or occupational designation from the bulk of the production workers; they differ only in their experience and the excellence of their performance of essentially similar tasks. In our sample, Type C is most closely approximated by a factory that produces oil engines and has 614 workers. It began its operations in 1947. It was preceded by a sister unit in the South Satara District to the south of Poona that still produces machinery and farm implements. The engine factory is clearly the most modern factory of all five in plant, production process, and organization. It, too, is a family enterprise, and the head of the enterprise is internationally known as a proponent of the most up-to-date Western style of factory organization for Indian factories. It differs from the other four factories in the relation of its workers to their machines. As we saw in the paper mill and the biscuit and rubber factories, each machine is fed, regulated, and serviced by a gang of workers who require very little skill except for minimal familiarity with the machine. In the textile mill, in the core of the production process—spinning and weaving—one worker tends one or more machines to assure that their repetitive processes proceed uninterrupted and at a maximal rate of speed. Only in the engine factory does the worker direct and manipulate his machine with any flexibility to produce a relatively complicated product. The machine, in effect, becomes his tool, and there is normally only one worker per machine.

We shall see in the chapters that follow how these three types of factories differ in their recruitment policies, the degree and nature of the commitment of their workers, and the internal organization of the workforce. We shall also see the extent to which each of these types shows a greater or lesser contrast with the surrounding non-factory social structure and thus promises to have greater or lesser "impact" on traditional social organization. Throughout the following chapters we shall refer to this typology as the production process typology.

We shall also encounter another typology that will coincide with a number of distinctions in the data. The factories fall naturally into two groups—old and new—

depending upon the date of their founding. The old factories—the textile and paper mills—were both founded
around the turn of the century. The new factories—
engine, biscuit, and rubber—were much more recent.
The engine and rubber factories were barely ten years
old at the time of the survey. The biscuit factory was of
about the same vintage or a little older, depending upon
whether the small pilot operation in another locality is
counted. This empirical typology has, of course, less theoretical relevancy but, as we shall see, it does coincide
with differences in the social "quality" of the workforces.
It will be relevant wherever the primary determining
factors seem to lie in the social characteristics of the
workers. The applicability of this typology will be examined in each instance. Here we need only note that it
provides a different clustering of our factories than does
the production process typology.

The Factory and the Traditional Society

The third major theoretical area of interest is allied to
the first. The "impact" of the factory upon the traditional
society is supposed to flow in part from the nature of its internal organization, which is presumed to be in sharp contrast to the social structure and culture norms of the surrounding society. Historical reconstruction of the pattern of
industrialization in the West supports a body of sociological
theory which views the long sweep of social evolution as a
transformation from one ideal type—"folk" society, *Gemeinschaft*, traditional society—to another ideal type—urban
society, *Gesellschaft*, contemporary society. The factory is
presumed to embody or promote the characteristics of the
latter ideal type, and it is from this contrast with the surrounding folk society that the harshness of its "impact" and

the potency of its catalytic function flow. Much of what was said above about the extreme contrasts chosen for study in the recruitment-commitment literature has relevance here, but there is, in addition, a highly developed theory of the presumed "impact" of industrialization. Throughout this literature, however, a relatively simple polarity occurs—a set of ideal types whose component parts appear again and again in discussions about changes from peasant to industrialized societies. For our purpose, we will select five changes which are presumed to accompany that process of social change called modernization: status is superseded by contract as the predominant basis of interpersonal economic relations; primary group organized production processes are supplanted by a more complex division of labor, finer job specification, and the interdependence of separate economic roles; ascribed status gives way to achieved status as the legitimizer of social gradations; status immobility surrenders to rapid vertical and horizontal mobility; and belief in the durability, inevitability, and propriety of one's status is replaced by aspirations for improving one's lot.

As with all ideal types, one is not likely to encounter an empirical example of one or the other polarity in pure form. Nonetheless, we do use many of these contrasts to bring order into our thinking about long-range changes in social organization, and many of our notions about the transformation from folk to urban, from *Gemeinschaft* to *Gesellschaft*, and from peasant to industrial societies draw their strength from these presumed parallel transformations.

The introduction of the factory is, of course, only one of the variables fostering this evolution. However, it is assumed that the introduction of the factory system has certain institutional imperatives that flow from this form of work organization, imperatives which are instrumental in

16

moving a society from one end of the polarity to another, from a static, acquired-status-ridden, tradition-bound, primary-group-oriented, particularistic, fatalistic society into one that is rapidly changing, achieved-status-dominated, progressive, secondary-group-oriented, universalistic and aspiring. In fact, the factory is presumed to embody the latter set of characteristics and thus, by its example, to upset the stable, traditional structure. It is the thesis of this book that "the factory" is a much more differentiated and gentle graft, that its institutional imperatives are not nearly so strong as might be imagined and that they are not moving in so orderly a fashion toward the modernization end of the polarity.[9]

But first a few words are required about the way in which the sample was chosen and the data collected.

SAMPLING AND DATA COLLECTION

At the time of the survey (January-March 1957) there were some 35 industrial establishments in Poona registered with the Government as factories.[10] However, most of them are small establishments at the workshop level. There is, in fact, a significant gap in the size distribution of industrial establishments between the small enterprises employing well under fifty employees and those with over one hundred. The gap is based in part upon the scarcity of the managerial skills necessary to transform the kin-like work organization of the small unit to the more bureaucratically organized larger unit. The lower cut-off point for inclusion

[9] Herbert Blumer makes the more extreme argument that industrialization merely provides a neutral framework for the operation of other factors. See his "Early Industrialization and the Laboring Class," *The Sociological Quarterly*, 1:5-14 (Jan. 1960).

[10] Under the Factories Act of 1948, a registered factory is an industrial establishment using power and employing ten or more workers, or if it does not use power, employing twenty or more workers.

in the survey was one hundred workers, and all but eight of the factories in Poona fell well below it. Of the remaining eight, three were owned and operated by the Government: a penicillin factory, a large complex of ordnance works, and a state transport workshop. A preliminary investigation indicated that the civil service aspect of the employment in these three plants dominated all other aspects of the workforce organization. It would be interesting to conduct a comparison of publicly and privately owned and operated factories in India, but it would require a different type of factory sample with more careful matching than was possible among the few manufacturing enterprises in Poona. Therefore, only the five privately-owned factories were chosen.

With the cooperation of the company managements, a stratified random sample was drawn from the attendance rolls of each company. In four of the companies, samples of approximately one hundred production and maintenance workers[11] were selected by the use of random numbers. Because of the greater size and complexity of the textile mill, one hundred and fifty of its P & M workers were drawn into the sample. For each factory, all the supervisors who were directly responsible for overseeing the daily work of other men were included. Administrative personnel were excluded. The term supervisor, then, should be taken in its literal sense. Clerks were drawn by a systematic sample from each company. The sample and total workforce of each factory is given below.

Each worker was interviewed in Marathi[12] at his home by

[11] Throughout the book, non-clerical workers below the supervisor level will be called production and maintenance (P & M) workers.
[12] The interview schedule, instructions to investigators, recording of responses and coding instructions were all in Marathi. At each stage, the material was translated from English to Marathi and in-

TABLE I

TOTAL WORKFORCE AND SAMPLE SIZE IN EACH FACTORY

Occupational Classes	Textile		Paper		Engine		Biscuit		Rubber	
	Total No.	Sample	Total No.	Sample	Total No.	Sample	Total No.	Sample	Total No.	Sample
P & M Workers	2173	158	536	111	539	103	129	98	473	102
Supervisors	84	84	38	38	22	22	12	12	13	13
Clerks	85	9	29	5	53	25	18	18	45	23
Total	2342	251	603	154	614	150	159	128	531	138

the author or a member of an interviewing staff composed of students drawn from the colleges in Poona.[13] One-tenth of the schedules were selected at random and reinterviewed independently to check upon the accuracy of the interviewing and the reliability of the response. There were in all only 14 refusals and 21 who could not be located at home out of the total sample of 856, giving a response rate of 95.9 per cent. The high rate of return can be attributed to a number of factors. The prestige of the Gokhale Institute of Politics and Economics and its reputation for impartial studies is extremely high, even among illiterate workers, and the support of the Institute was of tremendous assistance in overcoming suspicions. Prior to the beginning of the interview drive, copies of a letter requesting the worker's assistance and guaranteeing anonymity for responses were posted on bulletin boards throughout the factories. The letters were countersigned by officials of each company and by the leading union representatives. Finally, and not least important, the students conducting the interviewing

---

dependently back to English to ensure that the meaning would be constant from one language to the other.

[13] The interviews were under the over-all supervision of Shri C. S. Natu.

showed great ingenuity in explaining why an American professor should be collecting information on the work careers of Indian factory workers.

The interviewing period lasted from January to March 1957, and the data refer to the workforce at the time of interview. Those originally selected who were no longer in the factory were dropped from the sample.

Throughout the book, the data will be presented in a number of ways. When the entire workforce of a company, regardless of occupational grade, or some combination of data from one or more companies is to be presented, the data in each stratum will be weighed by the inverse of the sampling ratio before they are combined. This will have the effect of presenting the numbers and proportions as they would appear if the entire universe had been interviewed, and not just a sample. Within a single stratum of a single company, where the sampling ratio is constant, the original sample numbers will be used. Most descriptive statements will be of the former type, while the cross-sorting of variables will be of the latter type. The statistical data are presented in greater detail than would ordinarily be given because of the scarcity of empirical material in the field and the expectation that others will want to refashion these data for their own purposes.

In the following chapter, the social characteristics of factory workers in the combined workforce and in each of the factories separately will be compared with the adult male population in Poona. Chapter III will be concerned with problems of recruitment and commitment to the factory itself and the general operation of the labor market. Chapter IV will discuss the internal organization of each factory, its work and skill structure, and the amount of internal mobility noted in the workers' job history. Chapter V will relate the individual worker to the structure: examining the attributes which correlate with differences in hierarchical position and job careers, and exploring variations in aspiration level and degree of favorableness to the company. Finally, an attempt will be made to relate differences in the production system typology to the extent of the impact of "the factory" upon the traditional society.

CHAPTER II · SOCIAL
CHARACTERISTICS OF THE
WORKFORCE

▮:▮:▮ IF ONE VIEWS the introduction of the factory as a fairly radical innovation in a stable tradition- al society, one might reasonably expect that those drawn within its province would be a highly selective sub-set of the total population. Various notions about the nature of that selectivity are possible. One might expect with Slotkin that "new industrial employees become available from among those people who find their traditional culture inadequate,"[1] however their condition might be operation- ally defined in a non-redundant fashion. One might hold a more simple notion that those who were economically mar- ginal under the older system would move most quickly to the new opportunities, and thus factory workers would be drawn primarily from the lower echelons of society. One might anticipate that those unencumbered with family ties, or those who are young, or migrants into the city might make up a disproportionate share of the workers. One might expect that the literate and educated would find employ- ment in favorable positions in the non-factory society, and thus there would be a deficit of such people in the factory workforce. No matter which one or more of these notions dominated expectations of the domain of primary factory recruitment, one would not expect the factory workforce to be a representative cross-section of the surrounding society on those social characteristics which counted most in fixing a man's status. To put it more succinctly, one

[1] Slotkin, *From Field to Factory*, p. 33.

would anticipate that recruitment would be socially selective.

To determine the nature and extent of this selectivity, the factory workforce was compared with the general population of Poona on a number of simple demographic variables: sex, age, literacy, education, mother tongue, migrant status, ethnic group, and marital status.

THE CITY POPULATION AND THE FACTORY WORKFORCE

Sex

In the cities of India, particularly in the North, women make up a minority of the population, and an even smaller minority of the workforce. In Poona, females were 48.2 per cent of the total sample,[2] and only 15.3 per cent of the adult earners. In India as a whole in the year of this study, 1956, women represented 11.7 per cent of the working population in manufacturing industries, where they were concentrated in the medium and medium-large establishments.[3] Since the factories included in this study fall in the medium and medium-large classes, and since one of the factories, the textile mill, belongs to a category with a relatively high proportion of female workers—15.4 per cent— one might expect a substantial proportion of women in the factory workforce. However, only 30 females turned up in the sample, representing approximately 143 workers or 3.4 per cent of all the workers. Women were found in only two out of the five factories—the paper mill and the rubber factory—where they are over one-sixth and about 7 per

[2] Sovani, et al., *op.cit.* Except where specified, the data for Poona City are taken from this source. The sex distribution of the Poona population is given there in Table 1.17.

[3] *Occupational Pattern in Manufacturing Industries in India 1956,* Government of India, Planning Commission, 1959, Ch. 6.

cent respectively of the workforce. In manufacturing industries in India as a whole, a little more than two-thirds of the women were employed at unskilled jobs. In our factory sample all of them were. In the paper mill they sort the different grades of scrap paper by hand or carry heavy bundles on their heads, and in the rubber products factory they sort and pack the finished products. An occasional sweeper, *ayah*, or other domestics found in the other factories escaped our sample, but they have very little to do with the production process.

The 30 factory women are about evenly divided between those without husbands (15 widows, 1 divorcee) and those married (14). Only one of the women lives alone. Of the widows, one lives alone, 12 of them form a separate household with their own children, 1 lives with her parents and only 2 live in a household which includes her husband's relatives. The divorcee lives with her mother and her son's family. The women live in families slightly larger on the average than the rest of the factory workforce—4.9 members as compared with 4.2. Ten of the women are the sole earners in their family, but they do not seem to be in dire economic straits: the mean per capita income in all the women employees' families is actually higher than the general average—Rs. 35.4, as compared with Rs. 25.5 for the total factory workforce.

Age

It is impossible to make a detailed comparison of ours with the Gokhale Institute's data on age for two reasons. First, the class limits of the age groupings used in the two studies differ, and second, they have used a much larger open-end class (46 and over) at the upper end of their age

distribution.[4] While comparisons with the Poona population are difficult for the reasons enumerated, some contrast
with the age structure of the adult[5] males in the Poona
survey is possible, and it indicates that on the average the
factory workforce is somewhat older than the general population. The median age of the factory population is 32.4
years, while that of the adult males in Poona is only 28.2.[6]
Moreover, the proportion of the population in the older age
groups is higher for factory labor than for the Poona adult
males. In the factory sample, 13.1 per cent were 48 years
of age and over, and only 11 per cent were 46 and over in
the Poona sample.[7]

There are several factors which might make the workers
in the larger factories older than the surrounding adult
population. In the first place, it would be plausible to suppose that entry into one of the factories might have as a
prerequisite a previous period spent in a smaller establishment acquiring factory skills. This would leave in the
larger factories a proportional gap in the lower age levels.
A comparison of the individual companies, however, does
not show an association between age and level of skill
required by the factory. The more reasonable explanation
seems to be that fresh recruitment of workers is primarily
from younger age groups, but that the selective process of

[4] The age distribution for the entire factory workforce is given in
Table IX, p. 45.

[5] Adult is defined in the Poona study as 15 years of age and over,
which very closely corresponds to the age group in the factory.

[6] Since the Poona data are grouped in different class intervals, it
was not convenient to test the difference between medians for statistical significance by the usual method. The Poona medians were
calculated from Sovani et al., Table 1.6.

[7] No test of significance was used, but it will be noted that the
difference is understated because of the two year gap in the lower
limit of the age class.

turnover tends to make for an older and older age structure in the plant. Since a cross-section of the workforce at any given time includes mainly survivors from past turnover, the workforce tends to be old where turnover is small and the life-span of the factory exceeds the working life of a high proportion of its workers. That this seems to be the case is evident from a comparison of the marked variations in age structure among the factories, as will be shown later. For purposes of comparison it is interesting to note that the median age of 32.4 years found in this study matches fairly closely with the mean age of 30 years found in Niehoff's study of Kanpur factory labor.[8]

To return to our general theme, then, our opening speculation about the factories representing a younger age group does not appear to be true. When the factories were first introduced, they may indeed have drawn into their workforces primarily younger men, but the current cross-section does not reflect this tendency.

Literacy

To get some crude measure of literacy, each interviewer was provided with an identical set of newspaper clippings, one in Marathi, one in Hindi, and one in English. The worker was shown these three passages and asked to read them. The interviewer then rated the respondent's reading ability as none, low, medium, or high. After rechecking some of the ratings and a conference with the interviewers, we determined that the distinction between medium and high seemed to be too variable for reliable use and these two categories were then collapsed into one category called "high." The low category represented a halting, difficult

[8] Arthur Niehoff, *Factory Labor in India*, Milwaukee Museum, 1959, p. 33.

26

reading showing general comprehension of the content but an inability to render the text literally. All members of the interviewing staff were able to judge this rough division of reading ability in Marathi and English, but their knowledge of Hindi was so uneven that we decided to report only the presence, but not degrees, of literacy in Hindi.

TABLE II

LITERACY BY LANGUAGE AND DEGREE FOR ALL WORKERS
(Number of Workers = 4249)

Literacy	Per Cent
Marathi	70.6
high	57.6
low	13.1
English	25.1
high	17.9
low	7.2
Hindi	37.2
Any other language	3.1

In the Poona Resurvey 70 per cent of the adult male population not then enrolled in schools was recorded as literate. The Census of 1951 reported 73.0 per cent of the male population as literate. This is remarkably close to 73.1 per cent of the factory workforce displaying any literacy.

In view of the current stereotypes about illiterate factory workers in underdeveloped countries, it is somewhat surprising to find that almost three-fourths of the factory workforce is literate to some degree, with one-fourth literate in English. Even among workers below the clerical and supervisory level, 70.4 per cent are literate and 20.0 per cent literate in English. With almost no exceptions, literacy in English is a skill added to literacy in Marathi. One evidence of this is the much larger ratio of workers with low vs. high degree of reading ability in English as compared with Marathi. Therefore, those literate in English tend to be literate in at least two completely different languages. It is true that Poona stands high among the nation's cities in its educational system, but whatever the reasons, this is a reasonably literate workforce. In view of the national determination to establish Hindi as the lingua franca of the country, it is also interesting that more than one-third of the workers, 37.2 per cent, already have some literacy in Hindi. Of course, Marathi uses the Devanagari script as does Hindi, and Marathi is part of the same language family, but the dual competence is nevertheless striking.

Education

The surprisingly high literacy rate is, of course, a reflection of a more general characteristic—the educational history of the workers. Education is one of the primary bases of social stratification and is a fair index of the "quality" of the workforce or, to put it another way, the stratum of the population the factory is able to draw from. As with literacy, the workforce is more educated than most people would have anticipated.[9] About two-thirds of the workers have had at least a primary school education. Not too many years ago in the West this would have been a remarkably high percentage. Whatever economies are supposed to flow from an educated workforce should have at least begun to operate in the factories and, as we shall see when we examine the differences among the factories and the role of education in establishing the hierarchical posi-

[9] See for instance Niehoff's general statement that for Kanpur "the industrial workers as a rule have had little or no formal education and none of this group had attained college level." *Factory Labor in India*, p. 28.

tion of the worker in his factory, the workers have more education than most of the factories either need or are prepared to use.

In terms of the selectivity of recruitment from the general population, however, the educational profile of the factory sample in its general outline is not too far removed from that of the adult male population in Poona. While the

TABLE III

Per Cent Distribution of All Workers and Poona Population by Completed Education

Education	All Factories	Poona
No education	32.1	30.1
Up to 4th standard	30.5	20.2
Up to 7th standard	17.9	19.3
Up to 10th standard	10.3	13.0
Up to matriculation	6.2	11.4
Up to intermediate	1.6	0.7
Up to graduate	1.0	4.0
Up to post-graduate	0.1	1.2
No response	0.3	0.1
Total number	4249	7477

Poona Survey X all factories: $X^2 = 348.54$, df = 7, $p < .01$, C = .17. Poona data from Sovani, et al., Table 1.11, and include male adults who had completed their education.

difference is statistically significant, the fit is remarkably close: the Coefficient of Contingency is only .17, indicating a mild "relationship." As may be seen from Table III, about one-third in both the factory and the general sample have no education, and over 50 per cent have completed the 4th standard or less. What differences do occur indicate a higher proportion of factory workers in the lower educational categories, and gaps at the college graduate and post-graduate level. If the owners, boards of directors, managing agents, and top managerial staff had been included in the survey, the latter disparity might well have disappeared.

To the extent, then, that education measures social quality, the factories are not recruiting solely from the lowest social levels.

Caste and Ethnic Status

Further confirmation of this finding emerges from the data on the other primary determinants of social quality— membership in a caste or equivalent ethnic group. In view of the theoretical importance of the confrontation of the prototype ascribed and the prototype achieved status systems, caste and the factory, there are surprisingly few data available or, to my knowledge, little research in progress on the role of caste in the factory.[10]

We shall leave this general question to a later chapter, for here our concern is with the general social quality of the factory workforce as compared with the surrounding population. Each respondent was asked to specify his religion (dharma), his caste (jāt), and sub-caste (petjāt).

The question immediately arises as to what is the relevant unit with which to classify him, and what kinds of clusters of castes should be used. There are almost as many ways of speaking of caste as there are castes, and this is quite a few. For many purposes, the current practice of using as the basic analytical unit those groups known in Hindi as jāti, equivalent to the petjāt of the questionnaire and to the

[10] For a good summary of some of the relevant questions and the current state of information on the topic, see Morris D. Morris, "Caste and the Evolution of the Industrial Workforce in India," *Proceedings of the American Philosophical Society*, 104:124-133 (1960).

30

earlier English language literature as "sub-castes," is a fruitful one. Such an approach is especially useful in studying a local social system in India, such as a village, where there are a limited number of units, a good deal of face-to-face interaction, and a relatively slow rate of change. It is also useful in studying the origins of particular groups, the process of group amalgamation and fissure, or the peculiar sub-culture embodied within a particular caste. For the present study, however, the jāti must be grouped into larger classes to relate them meaningfully to the factory.

Ideally, broader categories of castes should be made on an ad hoc basis from combinations of these qualitatively separate units, and the classification should shift according to the nature of the particular variables used as the standard for the fundamental grouping. For instance, the jāti would be grouped one way, roughly in the older caste, sub-caste form, if the basic classifier was a combination of varna and traditional occupation or tribal affiliation. They would be clustered another way if urban vs. rural, degree of education, political power, or land-holding were the primary organizing principles. Unfortunately, no one has completed the type of empirical analysis of a large number of castes that would enable us to regroup the jātis in some more meaningful set of clusters than the general occupational and ethnic categories used by the census and most surveys.

Caste designations have been used in this study primarily as part of the general enquiry of whether the social organization of the society as a whole is reflected within the factory. This takes two forms insofar as caste is concerned. The question is whether the hierarchical ranking of castes parallels the hierarchical ranking within the factory. The second is more general; it asks whether a worker's caste or ethnic affiliation predicts his career and position within

31

a factory, whether vertically or horizontally. An example of
the first type of question will be whether or not caste
status rankings are positively correlated with wages or skill
grades. An example of the second kind will be whether or
not castes cluster in different factories, whether caste considerations enter into the hiring or promotion process,
whether the castes are differentially represented.

The first type of question demands a hierarchical ranking
of castes; the second type requires the treatment of castes as
separate, qualitatively different entities. In an attempt to
serve both of these purposes, the basic classification of
castes has been the one used by the Gokhale Institute. It
was developed as a status ranking system based upon the
consensus of expert judgment of all the members of the
staff. This has been modified to distinguish the village artisan castes, who might have some skills transferable to the
factory, from the village servant castes, whose skills seem
less transferable. This break corresponds approximately
with a status division as well, the artisans normally ranking
higher than the village servants. In the hierarchy, the precise dividing line between the categories is made difficult by
that fact that certain jāti under the same broad caste names
might fall into different categories. For instance, some Ramoshis might better be put into the Backward Castes category than be called Village Servants; Vaddars are originally
from Andhra, and the reported caste name of Pardeshi
literally indicates only that the caste had its origin outside
of Maharashtra. However, as far as possible, the Gokhale
Institute partitioning was followed.

To answer the second type of question another departure
from the Gokhale Institute classification was made. It was
felt that membership in a non-Hindu religious group or
origin in another linguistic area superseded specific caste

membership as a basis of group identification for an individual, and thus these two categories were taken out of the status gradation scheme and treated separately. Rough rank order, then, has been preserved for the Maharashtra-based castes, and people of other regions and other religions have been treated separately.

Many of the questions raised will be answered elsewhere in other chapters. The purpose of this section is to compare the caste and ethnic group distribution within the factory and the general Poona population to determine whether, as with education, the factory population is qualitatively selective in its recruitment. For this purpose, the castes and ethnic categories used in the Poona Resurvey were regrouped to coincide with the classification in this study. The full distribution of individual castes and ethnic groups for each factory separately and the Poona population is given in Appendix B.

On the whole, the match between the factory workforce and the Poona population is remarkably good for the broad categories. There is a slight deficit of Brahmans, particularly the elite Konkanastha, but this might have disappeared if the higher administrative staff were included. In any event, the deficit is replaced by the larger number of Marathas who make up more than a third of the factory workforce. The frequently noted verbal absorption of the large Kunbi caste into the Marathas is indicated by the infrequency of the term "kunbi" in both the Poona sample (16) and in the factories (14). Among the intermediate castes, the Malis are the most numerous, as they are in the general population. The disproportionately high proportion of Village Servants arises mainly from the high representation of Kolis, mostly in the textile and paper mills. The deficit of Christians, Jains, Parsis, Marwaris, and Sindhis is not sur-

TABLE IV

PERCENTAGE OF EACH CASTE OR ETHNIC GROUP IN THE
FACTORY WORKFORCE AND POONA POPULATION

Caste or Ethnic Group	Factories	Poona
Brahmans	15.0	19.7
Marathas	35.2	22.1
Intermediate castes	8.5	7.6
Village artisans	5.6	6.6
Village servants	6.8	3.3
Backward castes	11.2	12.5
Other regions	8.2	7.0
Other religions	9.3	15.5
No. in sample	821	5279[a]

Between all factories and Poona, $X^2 = 348.64$, df = 7, p < .01, C = .19.

[a] Source of Poona table is a detailed tabulation of caste and community provided to the author by N. V. Sovani, which was then reclassified into the present categories. 322, or 5.8 per cent, of the cases in the Poona sample were in miscellaneous caste groups that could not be redivided properly and they have been omitted.

prising in view of the specialized economic role normally played by these communities. It might have been anticipated that Muslims would have figured more prominently in the factory labor force, but they are in fact underrepresented. The Buddhists should really be added to the Backward Castes groups in that this was the remnant of the late Untouchable leader, Dr. B. R. Ambedkar's mass campaign to induce all Untouchables to convert to Buddhism. The Telegu, Tamil contrast is also an artifact of the particular timing of the two studies. The Poona Resurvey predated the creation of Andhra as a separate state, and Madras, now largely confined to Tamil speakers, at that time included the Telegu speakers as well.

In general the difference between the caste composition

of the factory workforce and the Poona population, while statistically significant, is surprisingly small. The "association," as measured by a Coefficient of Contingency ($C = .19$) is very mild. As in the comparison of education, it is again clear that the factories are not recruiting solely, or even largely, from the lower levels of society.

One reason why the factories can draw from the higher as well as the lower levels of society is that there are clearly a host of urban occupations less lucrative than employment in a large factory. In fact, the factory workers had higher average earnings than most of the adult male earners in the city. The Poona Resurvey showed a median annual income from all sources per adult male of about Rs. 828, and the median annual income from wages alone for the factory workforce was Rs. 1013.88. About 65% of the adult male earners in Poona earned less than the median wage of the factory workers. Even the unskilled factory worker, who is paid about Rs. 720 per year, is earning more than the income of one-third of the adult male earners in Poona. One might speculate that this situation had more bearing on the nature of recruitment than Slotkin's "cultural inadequacy."

The fairly good fit between the Poona and the factory caste profile disarms other substantive expectations that had some plausibility. For instance, on the one hand one might have anticipated that the artisans would have taken most naturally to the factory and would thus have been a disproportionately large group, or on the other hand that they would have clung to their traditional ways and thus resisted absorption into the factory production system. I have heard both views urged, but these data firmly support neither notion. It should be noted, however, that our data do not genuinely test either thesis, and that the amount of deviation between actual and traditional occupations

35

among artisan castes in the general population is unknown. Another presumption—that Brahmans are reluctant to enter so physical an enterprise as factory work—finds no support here. Nor do Backward Castes seem to be either excluded from or disproportionately attracted to the factories.

Migrant Status

One of our opening speculations, that migrants might provide a disproportionate share of the factory workforce seems to be true. The factory workers do have a much higher proportion of migrants from outside of Poona District than the Poona population—69.8 per cent compared to 47.3 per cent.[11]

However, the sources of migrants for the factories are not very different from those of the city population as a whole. In both cases between 50 and 60 per cent come from other districts of Maharashtra in the old Bombay State, excluding the areas in the former Madhya Pradesh. The relative importance of the Konkan, including Bombay City, and the Desh area of Ahmednagar, Satara, Sholapur, and Nasik is a little different; the city draws more from the Konkan than do the factories. Presumably migrants from Konkan to factories go to Bombay City and the pull of Poona for Konkan dwellers selects other segments of the population. The same relative shortage of migrants from North India in the factories is further indicative of selective pull. The greatest difference lies in the number of those

[11] In one respect our data do not appear to be as full as Sovani's. In both cases an attempt was made to distinguish between those born in Poona City and those from the surrounding rural areas within the district. In Sovani's survey this distinction lowered the percentage of non-migrants from 52.7 to 30.5 per cent. In our data, the drop was only from 30.2 to 30.0 per cent. It seems clear that many moves from the district into the city were not reported in our data, and we have therefore used Poona District as the native population in the table.

TABLE V

PLACE OF ORIGIN OF WORKERS AND THE POONA
POPULATION BORN OUTSIDE OF POONA DISTRICT

Place of Origin[a]	Per Cent Factory	Per Cent Poona
Desh	37.5	36.7
North Kannada	10.0	8.0
Konkan	15.3	20.3
Gujarat	1.3	3.3
South India	7.4	12.1
North India	10.6	15.9
Other places	6.8	1.1
No fixed place	10.6	1.6
Not stated	0.5	1.1
Number	2962	2365
Per cent of total	69.8	47.3

All factories compared with Poona: X^2 = 373.81, df = 7, p < .01, C = .22.

Source of Poona data, Sovani, et al., Table 2.1 with non-migrants added to Poona district figures. The Poona data refer to families.

[a] Desh includes Ahmednagar, Satara, Kandesh, Sholapur, Nasik. North Kannada includes Bijapur, Belgaum, Dharwar, Karwar. Konkan includes Ratnagiri, Kolaba, Thana, and Bombay City. Gujarat includes Surat, Broach, Baroda, Ahmedabad, etc. South India includes the former Hyderabad, Mysore, and Madras. North India includes the former Madhya Bharat, Madhya Pradesh, and the rest of India north of the former Hyderabad and Madras. All place references are to geographic regions prior to the reorganization of the states in November 1956.

who report themselves as having no fixed place of origin; the proportion is as high as 10.6 per cent for all of the factories and only 1.6 per cent in the city.

The distribution of mother tongues gives much the same picture. The per cent of Marathi speakers is 78.1 in the factories and 72.6 in Poona. Hindi and Urdu combined are next, followed by Telegu and Kanarese in that order. Gujarati represents 3.5 per cent in Poona, but less than one per cent in the factories.

37

TABLE VI

PERCENTAGE DISTRIBUTION OF MOTHER TONGUES
FOR ALL WORKERS AND THE POONA POPULATION

Mother Tongue	Factory	Poona
Marathi	78.1	72.6
Gujarati	0.7	3.5
Telegu	4.2	5.2
Kannada	3.6	1.9
Hindi	5.8	4.5
Urdu	4.2	7.0
Other	2.2	5.3
Number	4243[a]	5601

Marathi and non-Marathi speakers: all factories vs. Poona—
$X^2 = 40.33$, df $= 1$, p $< .01$, C $= .09$.
[a] One case in the sample did not report mother tongue.
The Poona data are drawn from Sovani et al., Table 1.5, and refer
to families.

Family

The basic element of social organization in India,
whether rural or urban, is still the family.[12] In contrasting
the family within which the factory worker resides and the
family clustering of the general population, we are interested not only in selectivity of recruitment—if Western
experience is followed one might expect factory workers
to have smaller families, a higher proportion of those never
married, and a high proportion of married males living
separately from their wives—but we also are interested in
the potential impact which the spread of the factory system
might have on the family structure of the society as a

[12] The term "family" in this and the Gokhale Institute study refers
to one or more individuals related by blood and living within a single
household. This is, of course, in many cases less than the effective
kin group which the term "family" should imply, but the outer edges
of this more extended group are undefinable in any way that permits
ready operational definition for enumerative purposes.

whole. In much of the discussion of the impact of industrialization on countries such as India, the most common assumption seems to be that one of the earliest influences of industrialization upon the traditional society is the disorganization of the traditional family.[13] Many of the changes predicted are qualitative changes not easily subject to measurement, but insofar as enumerative data are indicative of change, the factory population in Poona does not seem to differ radically or in the predicted direction from the general Poona population.

The factory workforce here is not composed of single males either by marital status or residence.

In the combined factory population, only 15.8 per cent have never been married, compared with 29.1 per cent among the adult males in Poona. The number of separations is higher than in Poona, 6.4 per cent as compared with less than 1 per cent in the general population, but is still a small proportion of all workers.

Not only are more factory workers married than is true for the general population, but the average size of family is greater—a mean of 5.2 members as compared with 4.5 for the Poona population. The primary test of an hypothesis that the factory is producing fragmented families should be the occurrence of a high proportion of factory workers who live away from their kin. We do not find this. In the factory workforce, the proportion of unimember families was only 5.4 per cent as compared with 7.2 per cent in the general population, and in no factory was the percentage as high as in Poona as a whole.

Of particular importance are the various attributes of

[13] For a list of such assumed changes see William J. Goode, "Industrialization and Family Change," in Bert F. Hoselitz and Wilbert E. Moore (eds.) *Industrialization and Society*, UNESCO-Mouton, 1963, Ch. 12.

TABLE VII

MARITAL STATUS OF ALL WORKERS IN FACTORIES
AND IN THE POONA POPULATION

Marital Status	Per Cent Factory	Per Cent Poona
Never married	15.8	29.1
Married with spouse	61.8	64.7[a]
Married separated	6.4	0.3
Widowed	7.4	5.9
Divorced	0.8	
Remarried	7.4	
Plural marriage	0.2	

[a] Includes remarried and plural marriage categories. Source of Poona data: Sovani, et al., Table 1.13.

the family as an economic unit, since differences in the economic composition of the family might well foreshadow other structural changes. There are several ways in which economic factors might make the composition of the families of factory workers differ from those in the general population. Heavy pressure of dependents might force an increasing number of members in the family into the labor force, raising the number of earners per family, or a factory worker with his relatively high income might attract dependents from other branches of the family less able to support themselves. Both processes seem to be taking place. We have already noted the larger size of the factory worker's family and the lower proportion of unimember families. It is also true that the mean number of earners per family is greater for all factories than in the general Poona population. This combination of larger families and greater number of earners per family tends to equalize the dependency load, bringing it very close to that in the general population—2.6 dependents per earner in the factory workforce and 2.5 in the general population.

TABLE VIII

EARNERS AND DEPENDENTS IN FAMILIES OF ALL WORKERS,
BY FACTORY

	Mean Number Earners per Family	Mean Number Dependents per Earner	Per Cent of Married Workers with Employed Spouse
All Factories	1.6	2.6	6.4
Poona	1.3[a]	2.5[b]	9.5[c]

[a] Sovani, et al., Table 1.17, total earners X 100 ÷ total families.

[b] Ibid., Table 1.17, total non-earners + unemployed X 100 ÷ total families.

[c] Ibid., Table 6.5, per cent of all families who have both male and female adult earners.

The hypothesis naturally arises that the greater number of earners per family is a result of a tendency of factory workers to have their wives work, but this does not appear to be the case. Comparison with the Poona data are not precise, since all that can be computed from the Poona Resurvey tables is the percentage of all families which have both a male and female adult earner. However, while this figure will be higher than the proportion of families in which both spouses are employed, it will include all such cases, and a substantially higher proportion of working spouses among men in the factory workforce would approach or exceed this figure. The evidence does not indicate that the factory workers are more likely to have working spouses than the general population—the proportions are 6.4 per cent and 9.5 per cent respectively.

Even where spouses are employed, the familial pattern gives no intimation of following the Western pattern wherein immediately after marriage both husband and wife work until child rearing removes the wife from the workforce. In our sample, it is not the young married men with the small families whose wives are employed, but the older workers with large families, perhaps driven by the pressure of mounting numbers of dependents and with families large enough so that the employment of both husband and wife does not disrupt their operation too much. The median age of those men whose wives are employed is 39.2 years, as compared with the median for all workers of 32.4 years. The average size of family of the men whose wives work is 6.4 persons, as compared with the average for all workers of 5.2 persons.

As we pointed out earlier, factory workers earn considerably more than most peasants and average about the same as the mean total family income of city dwellers. However, the factory workers' comparatively high income when compared with other non-self-employed earners in Poona is soon reduced when it is spread over the family on a per capita basis, making it about equal to the average for earners in Poona as a whole. The mean monthly per capita income of families of factory workers was Rs. 25.5, and for Poona Rs. 26.0.[14]

It is of interest to know to what extent the factory worker is carrying a dependency burden which would be reduced if his family were restricted to the form of unimember or conjugal family—worker, spouse, and children. Conversely, if the family organization of the factory labor force were to move toward the conjugal style of family, what would be the added burden of dependents that would have to be supported by the rest of the economy, given the ratio of earners to non-earners in the general population as at present? To estimate this, each worker's family's per capita

[14] The Poona mean was calculated from Sovani, et al., Table 1.19, by dividing the local earners' per capita yearly income by 12.

monthly income was recalculated using just the income earned by any members of the conjugal family and dividing it by the number of such members. This showed 67.7 per cent of the families would either increase or decrease their income if they became conjugal families.

With these as a base, we may examine the first of the questions. Those who would add to their per capita income an average of Rs. 21.78 came to 58.2 per cent, as compared with only 9.5 per cent who would lose an average of only Rs. 10.43. The net gain for all those whose per capita income would be altered would be Rs. 17.27, indicating that the non-conjugal members do constitute a financial burden on the factory workers. Precisely how much is still unclear because the amount is underestimated by including only those in the worker's immediate household.

The second question—the added burden on the economy with a change to the conjugal family—calls for the spreading of the gains over all the workers, rather than just the non-conjugal families. Derived in this way, the net burden would be Rs. 11.70 for each factory worker.

DIFFERENCES AMONG FACTORIES

While the factory workforce as a whole in its demographic characteristics matches fairly well with the general adult male population of Poona, this is not true if each factory is taken separately. There are, in fact, rather striking differences among the factories in the "social quality" of their workforces. Our first assumption was that these qualitative differences would correlate with differences in the relationship of the worker to the machine and his fellow workers, as characterized in the production process typology suggested in the introductory chapter. It quickly became

43

apparent that this division—which would have grouped the biscuit, paper, and rubber factories together as Type A and opposed them to the textile mill as Type B and the engine factory Type C—did not coincide with differences in the social characteristics of the workers. We then turned to the alternate typology given in the Introduction—an even less complicated division according to the length of time they have been in operation—to illuminate differences among the factories in their workers' ages, degree of literacy and educational attainments, caste and ethnic affiliation, migration history, and family characteristics. As we noted, upon the basis of duration of operation, the textile mill and the paper mill are grouped together as old factories, having been founded at roughly the same time around the turn of the century. The others are new factories, although in some characteristics the biscuit factory, founded in the 1930's, is mid-way between the new and the old. The significance of this age graduation of factories and its coincidence with differences in the social characteristics will be discussed for each demographic variable covered.

Age of Workers

In the two newest factories, the engine and rubber factories, each in operation less than 10 years, the workforces have median ages around 27 years, while in the older establishments, the textile and paper mills, the median ages of the workforces are around 35 years. The biscuit factory is mid-way with a median of 32.3 years. The same contrast among factories occurs in the relative strength of the upper age groups; the newest factories have 2.1 per cent and 5.1 per cent of their workers over 48 and the older factories have 18.0 per cent and 13.4 per cent over that age. The full age distribution is given in Table IX.

TABLE IX

PER CENT IN EACH AGE GROUP FOR ALL WORKERS, BY FACTORY

Age	Textile	Paper	Engine	Biscuit	Rubber	Total
13-17	–	0.8	–	0.8	0.9	0.3
18-22	7.0	4.2	8.7	9.1	26.6	9.4
23-27	14.0	21.0	47.1	21.5	26.9	21.7
28-32	21.3	18.4	19.7	21.4	24.3	21.0
33-37	17.2	14.0	12.6	17.0	8.5	15.0
38-42	12.6	13.5	6.6	15.4	4.8	11.0
43-47	9.9	14.8	3.2	5.6	3.0	8.6
48-52	8.1	5.3	0.4	5.6	4.7	6.0
53-57	7.9	5.1	0.8	2.3	–	5.3
Over 57	2.0	2.9	0.8	1.3	0.4	1.7
Number	2342	603	614	159	531	4249
Median age	35.2	35.0	27.4	32.3	27.2	32.4

$X^2 = 688.4$, $p < .01$, $C = 0.37$.

The different age structure of the new and old factories is clearly a byproduct of the retention of workers into the advanced ages in the older factories that have been established for a full generation, and does not represent either a recruitment preference on the part of the factory or a preference by the younger workers for the newer factories. This can be shown by restricting the comparison to those workers in the older factories who were hired during the period in which the newer factories have been operating, the last decade. The average age of workers hired during 1948-57 in the textile mill was 29.85 and in the paper mill 27.82, not appreciably different from the average age of workers in the newer factories who were all, of course, hired during the same time period.

Education

Education is a different matter. The factories do differ considerably in the educational accomplishments of their workers, as Table X indicates.

TABLE X

PERCENTAGE DISTRIBUTION OF ALL WORKERS BY
COMPLETED EDUCATION, BY FACTORY

Education	Textile	Paper	Engine	Biscuit	Rubber	Total
No education	39.2	43.9	11.1	14.9	16.6	32.1
Up to 4th standard	36.5	27.9	16.4	21.5	26.2	30.5
Up to 7th standard	15.8	17.5	19.6	29.8	22.2	17.9
Up to 10th standard	4.4	6.4	25.5	24.7	18.9	10.3
Up to matriculation	2.4	1.0	22.2	4.6	10.8	6.2
Up to intermediate	1.0	2.1	3.4	1.9	1.8	1.6
Up to graduate	0.7	1.2	1.1	1.9	1.7	1.0
Up to post-graduate	—	—	0.7	0.7	—	0.1
No response	—	—	—	—	1.8	0.3
Total number	2342	603	614	159	531	4249

Among factories: $X^2 = 958.69$, df = 24, p < .01, C = .43.

The factories recently established have the youngest workforces and also the greatest proportion of educated workers. In the engine, rubber, and biscuit factories 27.4, 14.3, and 8.2 per cent, respectively, of the workforces have at least passed the matriculation examination, and only from 11 to 17 per cent have no education at all. In contrast, in the paper and textile mills, a much higher proportion of the workers have no education—43.9 and 39.2 per cent respectively—and only about 4 per cent have passed the matriculation examination.

The coincidence of the higher educational levels for the three newest factories with the youngest age groups suggests several things. In the first place, the educational level of the Poona population has been increasing, and the educational differences may merely reflect differences in age distribution. In the second place, a somewhat allied process may be involved whereby the growth in the number of educated unemployed may be pushing more and more educated groups into the factories, thus raising the general educational level of the workforce. To examine these possibilities two types of comparisons were made.

Within the textile and paper mills, comparisons were made between those employed within the last ten years (as seen above an age group equivalent to that in the newer factories) and those employed in earlier decades. In both the textile and paper mills, those hired recently have more educational experience.[15] For instance, of the 1,065 workers hired in the textile mill in the past ten years, 28.6 per cent had no education at all, compared with 47.6 per cent of those hired earlier, and 39.2 per cent of the total textile mill workforce of 2,342 workers. In the paper mill, 27.9 per cent of the 190 workers hired within the previous decade had had no education, compared with 51.4 per cent of those hired before 1948, and 43.9 per cent of all workers.

The second comparison was made between the recently employed workers in the older mills and the full work force of the newer mills, that is to say, the hiring periods were held constant. Table XI indicates that the workforces in the newer factories are still more educated.

It appears that the educational level of the factory workforce in general is improving, but that the factories share unevenly in the change. In part, these inter-factory differences remain to be explored further; they are not solely a reflection of different skill requisites. While the engine factory demands the highest skill and has the most educated workforce, the rubber and biscuit factories demand little skill—certainly less than the textile mill. Nor do the factories uniformly differentiate among their

[15] Textiles: $X^2 = 91.81$, df $= 3$, p $< .01$, C $= .19$; Paper: $X^2 = 43.13$, df $= 3$, p $< .01$, C $= .26$.

TABLE XI

EDUCATION LEVEL OF WORKERS HIRED DURING 1948-57
IN OLD AND NEW FACTORIES

Education	Per Cent Old Factories	Per Cent New Factories
No education	28.5	13.9
Up to 4th standard	42.2	21.2
Up to 10th standard	24.6	44.9
Matriculate and above	4.7	20.0
Total number	1255	1294[a]

$X^2 = 347.38$, df = 3, p < .01, C = .35.

[a] Includes 10 cases whose education is unknown.

workers so as to utilize fully their educational qualifications, as will be seen in Chapter V. From the other viewpoint, it is not clear why the educated workers prefer to work for the newer companies. It is not wages, inasmuch as the biscuit and rubber factories have the lowest general wage levels and both rank high in the education of their workforce. It appears to be in part a result of the newness of the factories and their consequent better plant facilities. At any rate, in the labor-abundant market the choice lies primarily with the employer and, I suspect, in part at least is a matter of taste in that the family-operated concerns prefer to be paternal toward a labor force of a higher social "quality," and the primary guide to quality at the level of the factory worker is education.

Literacy

The same general picture which emerges from the data on educational attainments is shown in the literacy figures. Table XII gives the general literacy figures in Marathi, English, and Hindi for each factory.

TABLE XII

LITERACY AMONG ALL WORKERS BY LANGUAGE, DEGREE, AND FACTORY
(Percentages of All Workers)

	Textile	Paper	Engine	Biscuit	Rubber	All Factories
Any literacy	67.9	57.0	91.5	82.8	90.4	73.1
Marathi	66.9	54.6	84.0	82.2	86.3	70.6
high	50.0	39.8	78.8	73.1	81.8	57.6
low	16.9	14.8	5.3	9.1	4.6	13.1
English	10.4	21.7	63.6	46.0	46.7	25.1
high	8.4	15.7	45.5	19.2	33.6	17.9
low	2.0	5.9	18.0	26.8	13.2	7.2
Hindi – any degree	30.7	11.9	60.8	50.5	62.9	37.2
Total No. workers	2342	603	614	159	531	4249

As with education, the clustering of the two classes of factories is clear. The older factories, the textile and paper mills, have a much higher rate of illiteracy than the three newer factories. The most striking comparison is between the two factories at either end of the rural, unskilled workforce (paper mill) versus urban, machine-skilled workforce (engine factory). Less than 10 per cent of the engine factory workforce is illiterate while about half of the paper factory workforce is; almost two-thirds of the former is literate in English while less than one-fourth of the latter is.

Caste and Ethnic Status

As was noted earlier, together with literacy and education, the other chief guide to "quality" is caste. The full tabulation of workers by castes in each factory is given in Appendix B. Table XIII summarizes the differences among factories for the larger clusters of castes and ethnic groups.

Among the factories the Coefficient of Contingency is

TABLE XIII

PERCENTAGE OF ALL WORKERS IN EACH CASTE
OR ETHNIC GROUPS, BY FACTORY

Caste	Textile	Paper	Engine	Biscuit	Rubber	All Factories
Brahman	4.2	10.8	36.7	56.3	30.2	15.0
Marathas	44.8	29.2	20.7	23.6	19.6	35.2
Intermediate	7.9	10.4	6.0	5.8	12.6	8.5
Village artisans	7.3	2.6	6.1	3.7	1.8	5.6
Village servants	7.8	10.9	0.8	1.7	6.5	6.8
Backward castes	8.9	22.5	12.1	2.5	10.5	11.2
Other regions	9.7	5.9	5.3	5.6	8.6	8.2
Other religions	9.4	7.7	12.2	0.8	9.8	9.3
Total per cent	100.0	100.0	100.0	100.0	100.0	100.0
No. of workers	2342	603	614	159	531	4249

.41 ($X^2 = 876.64$, df $= 32$, p $< .01$), indicating a fairly high "relationship." The most striking difference is the high proportion of Brahmans in three of the five factories. In the biscuit factory, 56.3 per cent of the workforce is Brahman, in the engine factory 36.7 per cent, and in the rubber products factory 30.1 per cent—all well above the Poona proportion of 19.7. In contrast the paper and textile mills are only 10.8 and 4.2 per cent Brahman—well below the other factories and the Poona proportion.

Once again, this coincides with the dichotomy of the new and old factories. In general, the high proportion of Brahmans in the three newer factories seems to be a function of their demand for higher educational levels in their workforce (as will be shown later) rather than any specific caste selection, although what role if any is played by the fact that the three newer factories are owned and directly supervised by Brahman owners has not been determined.

50

The dichotomy of new versus old factories indicates differences in the proportions of other caste and ethnic groups. It will be noted that where the proportion of Brahmans is high, the proportion of Marathas is relatively low. The largest concentration of Marathas is in the textile mill, where they comprise 44.8 per cent of the workforce, although they are only 22.1 per cent of the Poona population. Those castes with village-based traditional occupations are more heavily represented in the older mills: Dhangars and Gavalis who are largely herdsmen by hereditary occupation; among the Village Artisans the traditional weaving castes of Sali, Koshti, and Vinkar as compared with the more urban Sonars (goldsmiths) and Shimpis (tailors) in the newer factories; most of the Village Servants—primarily Kolis, Bhois, Telis, and Ramoshis—are in the textile mill.

The scarcity of non-Hindus and members of low-status castes in the biscuit plant where food processing and handling is involved is not unexpected. The high proportion of Backward Castes in the paper mill is a result of the use of residents of a former Criminal Tribe compound near the factory as a supply of manual labor.

Migrant Status

As shown in Table XIV, a much higher proportion of the workers in all factories were born outside Poona than is true for the general population proportion of 47.3 per cent.

Within these uniformly high proportions, however, the division among factories again coincides roughly with new versus old factories, with the biscuit factory, somewhat older than the other two new factories, falling in the intermediate position. In each case, the bulk of the in-migrants came from Maharashtra proper, but some of the individual

51

TABLE XIV

PLACE OF ORIGIN OF WORKERS BORN OUTSIDE OF
POONA DISTRICT, BY FACTORY

Place of Origin	Textile	Paper	Engine	Biscuit	Rubber	Total
Desh	35.1	42.0	49.3	39.9	29.1	37.5
North Kannada	12.2	11.5	8.4	5.2	3.4	10.0
Konkan	18.0	6.4	12.1	23.5	15.1	15.3
Gujarat	2.3	—	0.2	0.9	—	1.3
South India	7.9	3.7	6.7	1.2	11.3	7.4
North India	8.6	12.0	6.0	10.6	21.8	10.6
Other places	9.3	—	5.8	5.5	4.9	6.8
No fixed place	6.6	21.5	11.4	12.1	14.4	10.6
Not stated	0.1	2.9	—	1.2	—	0.5
Number	1589	396	450	109	418	2962
Per cent of total	68.0	65.6	73.3	68.7	78.8	69.8

$X^2 = 364.83$, df $= 28$, p $< .01$, C $= .28$.

disproportions are interesting. While the data on past work experience will be presented fully in the next chapter, Table XIV does reflect in part the geographic spread of the recruitment area, or more properly, the area throughout which the previous experience of the workforce has been scattered. The narrowest geographic range of inmigration is in the paper mill, which tends to recruit its labor from the surrounding villages, and the widest is in the rubber factory. The heavy proportion of North Indian labor in the rubber factory is the result of deliberate recruitment, at high wages, of workers experienced in the manufacture of rubber products who have been brought all the way from Bengal and the Uttar Pradesh industrial areas.

Family Status

The most interesting aspect to emerge from the interfactory comparison of families is the way in which the considerable range in median monthly wages of the workers (column 1 of Table XV) evens out to a remarkable similarity, except for the engine factory, when it is spread across the resident family as a per capita monthly income (column 2), and the rather different family styles reflected in the subsequent columns and in Table XVI that create this uniformity. The mean per capita monthly income in the factory families would work out to about Rs. 300 per year. In the Poona Resurvey, the minimum annual income per adult unit so that "those who did not reach this standard suffered, in the light of generally accepted notions on the subject, from inadequacy of income," which they called the Poverty Line, was Rs. 600 per year in 1954; the Destitution Line was set at Rs. 240. These figures are not precisely per capita figures since women and children are counted as only fractions of adult units. In view of the uniformity of per capita income levels at a figure below the poverty line and the widely different family structures which all come to roughly the same average, one is tempted to wonder whether the household expands to the point where subsistence balance is reached and remains at that point. The notion is suggested by the data, but of course a much more rigorous study aimed at exploring precisely this point would be needed before even a hesitant conclusion could be reached.

The difference among the factories in family style can be gauged from Tables XV and XVI. In the latter Table it is clear that the newer factories have a much higher proportion of single workers. In both of the mills, the proportion of those who are either unmarried or separated is just below one-fourth, whereas in the other factories it ranges from 35.9 per cent in the engine factory to 59.1 per cent in the rubber factory. Variations in the "never married" category are partially explained by the younger age structures of those factories with high rates of single males. However,

TABLE XV

FAMILY CHARACTERISTICS OF ALL WORKERS, BY FACTORY

Factory	(1) Median Monthly Wage (Rs.)	(2) Per Capita Monthly Income (Rs.)	(3) Mean Number of Members	(4) Mean Number of Earners	(5) Mean Number of Dependents	(6) Per Cent Uni-member Families	(7) Per Cent Working Spouses
Textile	90.2	25.4	4.3	1.6	2.7	5.3	5.3
Paper	81.6	23.4	4.6	1.6	2.9	6.6	15.5
Engine	88.3	29.3	5.1	1.9	2.7	2.7	0.3
Biscuit	73.2	24.8	3.5	1.6	2.2	5.8	4.9
Rubber	61.6	24.1	3.6	1.9	1.9	7.0	4.4
All factories	84.5	25.5	4.2	1.6	2.6	5.4	6.4

TABLE XVI

MARITAL STATUS OF ALL WORKERS, BY FACTORY

Marital Status	Textile	Paper	Engine	Biscuit	Rubber	Total
Never married	8.9%	5.8%	32.6%	24.8%	35.8%	15.8%
Married with spouse	66.3	69.5	59.9	58.0	37.1	61.8
Married separated	7.0	4.5	1.0	6.6	12.2	6.4
Widowed	6.6	13.0	2.2	3.9	11.2	7.4
Divorced	1.2	0.8	—	0.8	—	0.8
Remarried	9.9	6.4	3.4	5.0	2.8	7.4
Plural marriage	0.1	—	0.8	—	0.9	0.2
Total number	2342	603	614	159	531	4249

when the separated and widowed are added, the truncated family emerges most clearly among the workers in the rubber factory, who not only have the highest proportion of never married but also the highest proportion of the separated and widowed, so that only 40.8 per cent of the workers are married and living with their spouses.

This appears to be a result of a combination of factors. Here we find the highest migrant rate—78.8 per cent of the workers migrated from outside Poona district; the youngest median age—27.2 years; a low median monthly current wage Rs. 61.6; and the lowest average seniority—4.5 years. In short, it is a young, newly recruited, relatively poorly paid workforce. By way of contrast, in the paper mill 69.5 per cent are married and living with their spouse. Its migrant rate is lowest—65.6 per cent, and much of its workforce is drawn from the nearby village areas; its median age is high—35.0 years; its mean current monthly wage is midway in an array of the five factories; and its seniority is high—15.1 years.

The marital status data, however, are not precisely parallel to the data in Table XV. For instance, while the rubber factory remains highest in the number of unimember families, the margin is considerably reduced, and the average in the paper mill is close to it. This is so because many of the single males in the rubber factory are living in a household with their kin. Comparisons of columns 3, 4, and 6 illustrate the differences in family style. The engine factory family has many members, many earners, an average number of dependents, but a very low rate of unimember families. The textile mill is about average on all counts. The rubber factory has a small family size, a high proportion of unimember families, many earners, and few dependents.

The remarkable aspect of the inter-factory comparison of working spouses (column 7) is the relatively high proportion (but still only 15.5 per cent) in the paper factory and the very low proportion (0.3 per cent) in the engine factory. If we look more closely at the paper mill, we see there were 21 in the sample who reported that their spouses were employed, and of these 8 were women. But even leaving the women aside, the rate is still high—9.4 per cent of the men in the factory having working wives. Contrary to what might be expected, this is not a case of family work groups in the factory. Only 4 out of the 21 had spouses employed in the paper mill, and in two of these both husband and wife were in the sample. Except for two Marathas, the men whose wives were employed were all low caste men—two Kaikadis, two Mahars, one Chambhar, four unclassified Harijans, a Bhat, and a Deccani Muslim.

SUMMARY

In general, the data showed that on the key social placement variables—caste, literacy, and educational achievement—the factory workers were not very different from a cross-section of the Poona population, and that on the variables where they did differ, the discrepancy was not in the direction one would anticipate on the basis of recruitment-commitment theory or Western experience. The workers were older, fewer of them were single, and they had larger households than the general population. The family data are especially interesting in that they measure one of the presumed consequences of industrialization: the growth of the small, nuclear family. Our data show just the opposite, that the relatively high income of the factory worker draws added dependents and thus larger families. Though the picture might be different in other sections of India, in this area, at least, factory employment does not result in an appreciable increase in the number of working wives. The percentage of workers whose wives work is probably lower than in the general population.

This general picture of a factory sample with the same social characteristics as the population at large, however, is not true for each factory taken separately. In fact, there seemed to be a time dimension at work. The factories were grouped by the recency of their establishment. The two older factories had been operating since the turn of the century—the textile and the paper mill. Two new factories were founded shortly after the end of World War II—the engine and rubber factories. A biscuit factory had been started in the 1930's. This time arrangement was reflected in sharp differences in the social attributes of the workers. The ages of the factories were paralleled by differences in the average ages of the workers, but this was mainly a result of seniority and turnover; the contrasts disappeared when cohorts hired during the past ten years were compared. The factories did differ on other major social placement variables—caste, education, and literacy; the newer the factory, the higher the "quality" of its workforce as measured by the per cent of Brahmans, literates, and high school and college trained. There seems then to be some trend toward drawing higher and higher levels of the general populace into the factory.

CHAPTER III · RECRUITMENT
AND COMMITMENT

▯▮▯▮ SO FAR we have viewed the problem of recruitment of a factory workforce largely in terms of
selectivity from the population which surrounds the factory.
In this chapter we will be looking more directly at the recruitment process itself, at the labor market as it is represented in the careers and attitudes of the workers, and we
will examine some data relevant to that elusive concept
"commitment," on the part of both worker and management.

It must be remembered, however, that the time when the
workers in our sample entered their present employment
stretches back over fifty years, and thus the aggregation of
their experience is not exactly the same as a cross-sectional
study of the labor market at one point in time. To uncover
any possible distortion resulting from this telescoping of
time differences, most of the variables discussed in this
chapter were checked for significant differences in the pattern among the various seniority cohorts. There does not
seem to be enough difference to make our merging of the
entire workforce unjust, except as specifically noted below.

PAST EXPERIENCE – ALL FACTORIES

The most extreme conception of the impact of the factory
upon the surrounding people envisages a population engaged largely in family-operated agriculture or handicrafts
suddenly thrust into a factory which subjects them to their
first experience of organized employment, time schedules,
machine operation, and so on. It is apparent to all, of course,
that this is an ideal-typical conception and occurs rarely in
fact. It is nonetheless relevant to ask to what extent any
factory must absorb people new to the labor force, and

58

socialize them to factory ways, in addition to training them for their particular tasks. This is important if only because socialization is part of the overhead cost of production and may have a good deal to do with differences in productivity. Tables XVII and XVIII indicate the extent to which the factories employ recruits who are new to the workforce, to the factory, and to the particular job for which they are employed.

TABLE XVII

PER CENT OF ALL WORKERS BY NUMBER OF
PREVIOUS EMPLOYERS, BY FACTORY

Previous Employers	Textile	Paper	Engine	Biscuit	Rubber	All Factories
0	28.4	58.5	40.2	33.2	51.2	37.4
1	41.5	22.0	24.7	35.9	34.5	35.3
2	16.5	15.2	20.2	20.8	7.4	15.9
3	5.0	1.0	7.7	4.8	3.9	4.6
4+	8.5	3.2	7.1	5.4	3.0	6.8
Number	2342	603	614	159	531	4249

We can immediately dismiss the notion that we are dealing with a peasant workforce. Only 28 out of the 821 workers in the sample indicated that they had ever been engaged in farming. The previous experience of these workers is almost exclusively in urban occupations. The exceptions were a few dairy farm employees listed under miscellaneous, an occasional village school teacher, and some handloom weavers listed under handicrafts workers. For that matter, as the first line in Table XVII indicates, a minority of them come to their present factories without some previous employment experience. Only 37.4 per cent have had no previous employers. From the third line in Table XVIII we

TABLE XVIII
Previous Experience of All Workers, by Factory

	Textile	Paper	Engine	Biscuit	Rubber	All Factories
Mean no. previous employers	1.34	0.68	1.19	1.16	.75	1.14
Factories among previous employers (%)	75.4	64.6	62.3	50.9	41.4	66.8
Workers have factory experience (%)	51.6	28.2	49.4	40.2	24.5	44.1
Experience in entry job (%)	36.9	10.5	32.4	26.6	15.9	29.5
Work experience in factories (%)	92.4	92.3	87.8	79.3	85.0	90.3

can see that almost half (44.1 per cent) of the workers had been employed in other factories before securing their present job. In fact, these two tables give some evidence not only of the extent to which the large factories pass on the socialization burden to smaller units and the non-factory sector, but conversely, may show the development of a specialized factory workforce.[1] Not that the mobility among units is very high—72.7 per cent had had no more than one previous employer, and the average number of previous employers was only 1.14. Nor do the large factories seem to exchange workers—only 21 workers in the entire sample reported having worked for another of the five factories, and 16 of these were ex-employees of the textile mill who were now scattered through the other four factories. It is clear from the last row of Table XVIII that the workers have spent almost all of the time in their work careers in

---

[1] It should be remembered that the nature of our sample does not permit the full measure of this specialization since it does not contain the possibly important group who were once in the factories and have now left it for other types of employment.

factories.[2] From about 80 to 90 per cent of the labor force time of the workers in each factory was spent in factories, and about two-thirds (66.8 per cent) of the places of previous employment could be classified as factories. The prevalent factory background of the workers in our sample, however, does not imply that the training for the specific jobs for which the workers were hired was generally done elsewhere. Only about 30 per cent of the workers brought to their current employment direct experience in the job they performed on entering the new firm.

Having concerned ourselves with the amount and degree of experience of the workers within the factories in our sample, it is now of interest to distinguish the types and the range of work experience represented by this one limited sample of factory labor. Table XIX indicates within each factory the percentages of previous employers who were engaged in the specified economic activities.

The job histories of the workers present a truly remarkable spread of employers. There were in all 431 different employers mentioned. Here is a partial list just to give some of the flavor of the range of previous employers: ink factories, domestic service, oil mills, cinema houses and studios, sugar factories, newspapers, laundries, tea companies, hospitals, public works departments, banks, police, military, railways, schools, grocery stores, hydro-electric supply companies, dispensaries, bus lines, hotels, stone cutters, air lines, bidi works, bakeries, docks, pan shops, soap factories, tonga-wallas, cycle marts, law journals, pleaders, ayurvedic medicine factories, tire makers, fire brigades, cement factories, chemical factories, insurance companies, lumber companies,

[2] The figures in this row are derived by dividing the total seniority in the labor force for each worker into the total time spent in factories (including the current employment) and taking a mean.

61

TABLE XIX

PER CENT OF PREVIOUS EMPLOYERS IN EACH
TYPE OF ENTERPRISE, BY FACTORY

	Textile	Paper	Engine	Biscuit	Rubber	All Factories
Textile mills	46.5	24.3	6.4	5.9	8.6	23.0
Raw material processing	2.5	8.1	5.5	22.1	17.2	8.8
Metals and engineering	3.1	8.1	20.2	5.9	3.4	8.3
Other heavy manufacturing	15.8	8.1	14.7	4.4	8.7	12.1
Transport and power	7.5	8.1	13.8	8.8	6.9	9.3
Construction	1.9	—	5.5	2.9	3.4	3.0
Handicraft	3.1	8.1	1.8	—	—	2.3
Government	6.9	2.7	12.8	13.2	24.1	11.4
Retail sales	7.5	13.5	4.6	17.6	10.3	9.3
Education	—	8.1	0.9	7.4	5.2	2.8
Newspaper and printing	1.9	2.7	2.8	2.9	5.2	2.8
Miscellaneous	3.1	8.1	11.0	8.8	6.9	7.0
Number of employers	159	37	109	68	58	431

and the telephone exchange. All of these have been mentioned more than once, and the full range is even broader.

The most heavily represented among the previous employers were textile mills, reflecting in part the predominance of this industry in India as a whole and more particularly in Western India. There were in all 99 different textile firms in the work experience of the 821 workers in the five factories sampled. Aside from the surprisingly high figure in an absolute sense, it is also interesting to note that the workers in the sample have worked in roughly one-fifth of all the 511 textile mills in India. In fact, the workers in only one factory, the textile mill in Poona, have worked in 75 different mills, or a little less than a sixth of all the textile mills in India.

Another previous employer that appears frequently (81 times) in the employment record of the workers in the sample is the government arsenal and ammunition factory in the industrial suburbs of Poona. Workers from this large industrial complex are found in all five factories.

The sources of experience of the factory workers are not only distributed widely throughout the various economic categories, but geographically as well. It will be recalled from the previous chapter that some 69.8 per cent of the factory workers had been born outside of Poona. To put the following discussion in the proper frame of reference it must be pointed out that 68.1 per cent of the workers had spent their entire *factory* career in Poona. Nonetheless, the geographic spread of previous employers was considerable. More than half (53.6%) of all 431 previous employers were outside Poona (Textile 74.6%, Paper 62.2%, Engine 40.4%, Biscuit 23.5%, Rubber 50.0%). These previous employers were distributed throughout some 73 different towns and cities. Table XX indicates the location of the previous employers.

TABLE XX

LOCATION OF PREVIOUS EMPLOYERS

Location	Textile Mills (Number)	Other Employers (Number)	Total (Per Cent)
Poona	1	199	46.4
Bombay City	61	53	26.5
Other Maharashtra	12	52	14.8
Gujarat	9	8	3.9
Mysore	6	4	2.3
Other	5[a]	14[b]	4.4
Unspecified	5	2	1.6
Total number	99	332	431

[a] Indore (2), Secunderabad (1), Karachi (1), Gwalior (1).
[b] Calcutta (3), Asansole (1), Indore (4), Rajamahendri (1), Allahabad (1), Karachi (1), Lahore (2), Iran (1).

Several features can be observed in Table XX. The over-whelming majority (87.7 per cent) lie within the linguistic region of Maharashtra—Poona, Bombay City and other Ma-harashtra—and a full quarter of the employees have worked in Bombay City itself. Neighboring Gujarat and Mysore make up another 6 per cent. In fact, only 4 per cent of the employers lie outside this region of Western India. Within the Maharashtra area, however, there are 35 different towns represented, from Nagpur on the east to Ratnagiri on the west, and from Ahmadnagar in the north to Kolhapur in the south. The spread of those outside the Western India area is indicated in the footnotes to the table. It reaches to Pakistan, and even to Iran, where two workers served with the Anglo-Iranian Oil Company.

The concentration of textile experience indicates the ex-tent to which the Poona mill is dependent upon other units in the industry for the training of its labor force. Its workers have been employed in 61 out of the 65 textile mills in Bombay City, and they also come from the subsidiary textile centers such as Ahmedabad and Surat in Gujarat, and Sholapur in Maharashtra itself, reaching in all 84 out of the 211 other mills in the former Bombay state.

Past Experience–Among Factories

A glance back at Tables XVII and XVIII will indicate that, as in the case of the social characteristics of the work-ers, the composite picture of the workers' experience for the combined factory workforce is made up of somewhat vary-ing occupational histories for the employees in each factory. We may start the analysis by asking to what extent our production process typology is reflected in differences in the amount and type of experience a factory commands as a prerequisite to employment. We would expect that the

Type A factories—with their simple gang machine-tending and two- or three-stage production processes—would need few skills in their new recruits and that the socialization process of raw workers would be relatively easy. This expectation is generally fulfilled. More than half the employees hired by the paper mill and the rubber factory, both Type A, had no previous experience of any kind. Only about a fourth of them had previous factory experience, and only from 10 to 15 per cent were experienced in the work for which they were employed. The biscuit factory, however, is also a Type A factory, and although its skill demands are no greater than those of the rubber and paper factories, it recruits slightly more experienced workers. This is so because there are many other units in the food processing industry not too far away, while there are no other units of the paper or rubber industry nearby. (The rubber factory had to go all of the way to Calcutta to get a few experienced workmen for key positions in the company.)

All three factories, however, have relatively low experience demands when compared to either the textile mill (Type B) or the engine factory (Type C). In both the latter, skilled workers, although their skills are of a contrasting character, can be used directly in production. Both factories hire about a third (36.9 and 32.4 per cent, respectively) of their recruits with previous experience in their entry jobs, and in both cases about half have had previous factory experience. The contrast between the two factories is in their willingness to recruit and absorb workers with no previous employment experience of any kind: the engine factory took in 40.2 per cent without previous experience, while the textile mill took only 28.4 per cent. The difference seems to lie in the amount of socialization they are willing to undertake. This will be evident when we discuss the internal structure in these factories in the next chapter. Here it is only necessary to say that both factories recruit directly relevant skill when they can get it. When either entry job or factory experience is lacking, the textile mill tends to insist on previous work experience of some kind, while the engine factory is willing to substitute higher educational qualifications for work experience.

Looking back at Table XIX, we see some evidence of specialization of previous experience, or to put it another way, workers seeking new jobs move to factories in the same general category as those for which they have worked. The concentration in the Poona mill of workers with previous textile mill experience has already been mentioned. The biscuit and rubber factories engaged in raw materials processing have a relatively high proportion of the previous experience of their workers in this category—mostly first-stage processing of agricultural products, such as oil pressing mills, flour mills, tobacco processing. The engine factory draws its experienced workers mostly from heavy industry such as metal manufacturing, engineering, transport, and power. The higher proportion of former government employees in the newer factories—the engine, biscuit, and rubber factories—is a result of the higher educational level of their workers. But aside from these tendencies toward concentration of occupational experience, the range within each factory is wide.

THE WORKER IN THE JOB MARKET

In view of the facts that (1) India is a labor surplus economy; (2) that Poona in particular had an unemployment rate of 9 per cent in 1954, up from 3 per cent in 1937; (3) that the nearby ordnance factory had just laid off 5000 workers who were desperately and, by and large, unsuccessfully seeking jobs at the time of the survey; and (4) that, as we have pointed out, factory jobs are relatively high-paying, steady, and sought after compared with many other ways of making a living in Poona—in view of all this, one might expect that job histories of the factory workforce sample would reflect some difficulties in obtaining factory work and some periods of unemployment. To the contrary, most workers reported little difficulty in finding their first job. Thirty per cent of the workers in all factories reported getting their first jobs as soon as they wanted them. The median time spent in search for the initial job was only two months. Nor have the workers been plagued with unemployment. Two-thirds (66.8 per cent) of all workers reported no unemployment period whatever since they first secured a job. The minority who had been unemployed had a median time spent without work of only 10.7 months. Of those who were unemployed, only 2.4 per cent reported more than one period of unemployment.

In view of this relatively secure job experience, little anxiety shows up when the workers contemplate the loss of their present jobs. It should be pointed out that the questions asked in this regard were necessarily hypothetical, and sentiments would no doubt be less calm if the threat were more realistic. Nonetheless, the sanguine attitude toward even this hypothetical event is striking. Only 2.4 per cent of all the workers foresaw an indefinite period of unemployment if they were to be laid off. About one-third (36.1 per cent) could not estimate how long they would be unemployed, but did not think it would be "too long." Of those who gave a time estimate, 8.9 per cent indicated they could get another job immediately, the others expected that the median time spent in the search was to be only three to four (3.7) months. Only 10.8 per cent thought it would take more than a year to find a new job. Not only did the workers expect only a brief period of unemployment, but only 28.3 per cent felt that it would be difficult or impossible to get a new job, and as many as 29.8 per cent were reasonably sure that the search would be easy.

The factors which increase the workers' sense of security in operating in the job market are not clear. Among the factories, it was the workers in the highly skilled engine factory and textile mill (Type C and Type B) that had the most optimism: 43.2 per cent and 30.8 per cent of their workers estimate that they would easily find a new factory job in case of retrenchment, as compared with 28.8, 23.8 and 18.5 for the biscuit, rubber, and paper factories (all Type A). It was also true that in every factory the percentage expecting no difficulty in relocating was appreciably higher for supervisors than for production and maintenance workers. This would seem to indicate that increasing skill leads to an increasing sense of security in the labor market. Unfortunately, however, in none of the factories is there a significant correlation between the skill levels among the P & M workers and the percentage who expected little difficulty in finding another job. Nor do other variables that might be expected to influence a worker's estimate of his chances in the labor market appear to distinguish the optimists from the pessimists. Leaving the supervisors and clerks aside, we divided the P & M workers in each factory into two groups: those who thought that finding a new job would be difficult or impossible, and those who thought it would be easy. In none of the factories did these two groups differ significantly as to age, the proportion of skilled versus unskilled, education, or even the number who held previous employment or previous factory jobs before joining their current factory.

68

The data, therefore, do not clearly reveal any factors which produce differences in the workers' sense of security in the Poona job market. At this point, all we can say is that if the data have any meaning at all, it is a negative one: that is, that variables which would be expected to affect a worker's chances of securing a new job if he were laid off, such as age, education or skill, do not seem to influence his own estimate of his chances. Perhaps we should have examined his kin network. The contrast among the factories does suggest that there is some sense of participation in industries with several alternative outlets for skills acquired in the present factory. Hence, the higher degree of optimism in the engine factory and textile mill which, as was pointed out earlier in this chapter, are the two factories that hire the most P & M workers with experience directly relevant to their entry jobs. The greater sense of security among the supervisors may be related to the genuine shortage of workers with middle-echelon supervisory experience.

Our data are equally unsatisfactory for unearthing the reasons for job changes when they do occur. It will be recalled that for 37.4 per cent of the workers, the present firm had been their only employment. For the others, entrance into the company for which they now worked was their second, third, or even in four cases in the sample, their tenth job. It is difficult to analyze the relative weight of the reasons for their job changes. When asked, the workers most frequently gave some equivalent of "retrenchment"[3] as the reason, but in such vague terms and with such added reasons as "I had to move to Poona" or "I was offered a permanent job here" that a much more thorough investigation of job-change motivations would be required before

[3] The word commonly used in India to mean an involuntary layoff when the company is reducing its workforce because of lack of business.

69

any firm statements could be made on this matter. There are two negative statements that can be made, however, which will help to narrow the range of future research. One indication of whether or not the job changes were due to economic attraction would be the relative wages of the job that was just left and of the entry job into the present company. If the attraction of higher wages were a predominant influence, one would expect that the new wage in most cases would be higher than the old one. In point of fact, the superiority is distributed about evenly among the jobs. For all entries into the present companies which involved job changes, just over half (51.7 per cent) involved an increase in wages, about forty per cent a decrease, and ten per cent the same wage. There is little difference among the different factories in these proportions, and one is tempted to say that wage differences occur at random in job changes. Nor does the change appear to have been traumatic in the sense that the workers were thrown upon their own resources for any length of time. Only about 20 per cent of the job changes caused any appreciable period of unemployment, and this figure is relatively consistent from one factory to another. This is not to say that most workers who leave a job do not have a period of unemployment, for we would need a full sample of departees to answer that question. What we can say is that those who find jobs in large factories tend to do so in a fairly short period of time after leaving their old jobs.

ENTERING THE FACTORY

How do the workers find out about and gain access to the new jobs? In Western societies, this operation has come to involve a set of formal mechanisms that serve both to screen applicants and to facilitate entry into a factory. To test the operation of these mechanisms in the Poona factories, each worker was asked whether he had submitted a written application, had answered a newspaper advertisement, had been directed to the job by a union, or had utilized the services of the government-operated employment exchange. In Poona there are no effective private employment agencies of the kind usually found in Western cities. Table XXI describes the use of these formal mechanisms in securing the workers' present employment.

TABLE XXI

PERCENTAGES OF WORKERS ASSISTED BY FORMAL CHANNELS
FOR SECURING JOB, BY FACTORY

Channel	Textile	Paper	Engine	Biscuit	Rubber	All Factories
Written application	9.7	9.3	52.1	59.8	19.9	22.1
Newspaper advertisement	0.7	1.8	3.8	21.1	1.8	2.2
Union	0.6	15.6	—	1.7	2.6	2.9
Employment exchange	0.6	0.2	11.1	0.8	1.8	2.2
No. of cases	2342	603	614	159	531	4249

The use of formal mechanisms is one way of impersonalizing the labor market, a process which in the West was deemed to be essential to the full growth of an industrial system. It is clear from Table XXI that this process has not proceeded very far in India, in these factories at least. The only formal mechanism that was used to any extent was the written application—22 per cent of all workers submitted written applications—and this device plus the newspaper advertisement are clearly a literacy screen. The use of the union in the paper mill is a result of the personal influence of some union officials rather than a use of the organization itself. While in some other cities and industries, notably in

71

the textile industry in Bombay,[4] more progress has been made, in Poona, as Table XXI and the following discussion will make clear, the traditional system has been only partially abandoned. The one exception is where we would expect it, in the Type C factory where formal screening devices, including the employment exchange, were utilized by the company in filling its job openings.

Because of the special interest in the use of the government employment exchanges in the large factory sector of the economy, an additional probe question was asked to see whether any of the workers had enrolled with or had ever known another worker who had secured a job through the employment exchange. The probe question was intended to see whether the limited activities of the exchange were reaching the workers at even one step removed.

It can be seen that only 6.7 per cent of the workers were ever helped or knew of someone who was helped by the exchanges.[5]

The differences in enrollment among the factories reflect two sets of factors. In the first place, the employment exchanges are new (established in 1945), so that workers who have been steadily employed since before 1945 are not likely to have been enrolled. The differences in use among the companies, therefore, reflect the different seniority distributions within the factories. The other set of factors relates to the social characteristics of the work force. As Sovani points out, it is the younger, more educated people in the population who use the exchanges. Such people are

[4] Ralph C. James, "Labour Market Insulation and Technical Change: Rationalisation in Bombay Cotton Textiles," *The Economic Weekly*, Vol. XI, Nos. 4, 5, 6, January 1959.

[5] A useful survey of the Poona Employment Exchange is covered in Sovani, et al., *op.cit.*, pp. 332-353.

TABLE XXII

Use of Employment Exchanges by All Workers, by Factory
(Per Cent)

	Textile	Paper	Engine	Biscuit	Rubber	All Factories
Ever enrolled	13.0	14.9	58.3	29.8	51.6	25.2
Ever helped	0.6	0.2	11.1	0.8	1.8	2.2
Not helped, knew some- one who was helped	3.4	3.5	9.9	9.3	2.7	4.5
No information	—	0.8	—	—	0.9	0.2
No. of workers	2342	603	614	159	531	4249

proportionately more numerous in the newer factories (engine, biscuit and rubber).

To explore further the use of employment exchanges, the data for the engine factory, our Type C factory, were analyzed more intensively. In addition to the fact that this factory most closely resembles the Western mode of skill organization, it also had the largest number of workers who had been enrolled with the exchange, and, since the factory had been opened well after the establishment of the Employment Exchange in 1945, all workers would have had an opportunity of registering before joining the engine factory.

Several conclusions emerge from an examination of these data. First, the fact that the engine factory had the highest proportion of workers who had enrolled with the Exchange appears to be evidence of the more frequent use of the Exchange by skilled workers. This hypothesis is borne out by an examination of Table XXIII, which shows that a higher proportion of the P & M workers hired above the unskilled level were enrolled with the Exchange. For per-

TABLE XXIII

Use of Employment Exchanges for All Permanent Workers
of Engine Factory, by Occupational Class of
First Job in Company

| | Enrolled | | Assisted | | All |
	Number	Per Cent of All Workers	Number	Per Cent of All Workers	Workers (Number)
Unskilled	131	45.8	—	—	286
Skilled	142	75.1	39	20.6	189
Supervisors	2	33.0	1	16.7	6
Clerks	19	43.2	2	4.5	44
	294	56.0	42	8.0	525

manent workers, the coefficient of contingency is .52 ($X^2 =$ 10.23, df $= 1$, p $< .01$). That this greater use of the Exchange by the skilled workers is not without a logical base can be seen by noting that almost all (39 out of 42) of the workers who reported that the Exchange had assisted them in finding a job were hired at jobs above the unskilled level.[6] However, even at this level, only 20.6% of all who were hired at this level were assisted by the Exchange. Clerks and supervisors were rarely hired in this way. The determination of skill at the time of employment does not rest entirely upon previous experience, however. If skill at time of hiring meant experience, one would expect that those holding previous jobs would be more likely to appear among the enrollees than the workers for whom the engine factory was the first employer; more directly, that those who had worked in factories would be more likely to be among the enrollees; or even more directly, those who had

[6] No entry job was distinguished for temporary workers. These figures do not include supervisors and clerks.

worked elsewhere in a related or the same job as the one for which they were hired. None of these relationships was significant.[7]

The other variable is, of course, education. Out of 25 workers in the sample who had enrolled with the Exchange but who had held no previous jobs, 16 had completed the 10th standard or more. More generally, Table XXIV shows the distribution of those enrolled and those not enrolled by educational category, and shows that the more educated workers are more likely to have registered with the Exchange.

Aside from the registration, those actually assisted by the Exchange in securing jobs tended to be both educated and experienced. Of those who were assisted by the Exchange, 58 out of 68 had up to 10th standard or more in education, and 46 out of the 68 had had previous job experience.

If the formal channels of securing a position are used infrequently, what, then, are the mechanisms by which

TABLE XXIV

ENROLLMENT IN EMPLOYMENT EXCHANGE IN SAMPLE
OF P & M WORKERS IN ENGINE FACTORY,
BY EDUCATIONAL LEVEL

Education	Enrolled	Never Enrolled	Total
No education	3	10	13
Up to 4th	11	8	19
Up to 7th	15	7	22
Up to 10th	19	8	27
Matriculation and over	16	6	22
	64	39	103

$X^2 = 10.74$, df $= 4$, p $< .05 > .01$, C $= .41$.

[7] The relationships were tested for the permanent P & M workers only, since no entry job had been asked of the temporary workers. No supervisors or clerks were included in the computations.

jobs in the factory are sought? Since India is a classic case of a particularistic society, to use Talcott Parsons' term, in that it is not *what* you are but *who* you are that counts, the answer is not surprising. The workers were asked what they thought was the most important factor in securing a good job. *Vashilā*, which is an almost perfect translation of the English slang "pull" or influence, was cited by 50.2 per cent.[8]

TABLE XXV

JUDGMENT OF THE IMPORTANCE OF INFLUENCE IN GETTING
A GOOD JOB FOR ALL WORKERS, BY FACTORY
(Per Cent)

Relative Importance	Textile	Paper	Engine	Biscuit	Rubber	All Factories
Most important	47.7	60.2	55.9	31.1	49.2	50.2
Important but not most	31.6	19.5	27.9	46.9	34.3	30.3
Counts some but not much	7.2	6.9	11.9	10.0	9.5	8.2
Not at all important	11.1	12.7	4.2	12.0	7.0	9.9
No response	2.4	0.8	—	—	—	1.4
Number of workers	2342	603	614	159	531	4249

Only about 10 per cent of the workers were willing to say that "influence" was not at all important, and more than 80% felt that it was either the most important or that it was very important. Among the factories, there is a significant difference ($X^2 = 117.30$, df = 12, $p < .01$) but only a mild "relationship" ($C = .16$). What differences do occur among factories are a result of differences of opinion as to whether influence is the most important factor or only one

[8] The Marathi question was "cāglī nokarī miḷnyāsāṭhī vashilā āvaṣyak āhe asē tumhās vāṭṭē?" The multiple choice responses were: "vashilā sarvāt mahattvācā"; "vashilā mahattvācā kharā paṇ itar goshṭīnāhī mahattva āhe"; "vashilyācā thodāsā upyog hoto"; and "vashilyācā bilkūl upyog nāhī."

of several important factors in securing a good job. If these two categories are collapsed, between 78 and 84 per cent of the workers in each factory would agree to the importance of influence.

For many years the classic way of gaining influence was the payment of "dasturi" or a petty bribe. The Labor Commission reports and other investigations of labor conditions condemned this practice as one of the greatest burdens upon the workers. In part to eliminate this practice, the hiring and firing powers of lower echelon supervisors were removed. Whatever its history, few of the workers in the Poona factories felt that it was important today, or more specifically, that they would be able to get a better job if they had some money to spend, and 89.2 per cent stated positively (sometimes forcefully) that money would not help. Even those who thought it would help could not agree upon the amount. While the mean was Rs. 95 for those who gave an estimate, the range was great—the coefficient of variation was 90.1, that is, the standard deviation was almost as large as the mean.

Rather than money, the key to the influence pattern is the same as it is in the society at large. The extended family and acquaintance system gives a worker a network of relatives and friends who feel some obligation to assist him in his job search. The following tables show the nature and position of contacts within the factory which the workers had at the time they joined the company, and the type of assistance rendered by them.

For all companies, two-thirds (67.7 per cent) of the workers already knew someone in the factory when they were first hired, and 84.4 per cent of these friends and relatives appear to have given the prospective employee assistance in securing his job. In more than half of these

TABLE XXVI

CONTACTS[a] IN FACTORY AT HIRING TIME FOR ALL WORKERS
BY OCCUPATIONAL CLASS OF CONTACT, BY FACTORY
(Per Cent)

	Textile	Paper	Engine	Biscuit	Rubber	All Factories
Supervisors	19.6	20.1	21.6	7.5	23.4	20.3
Relatives	2.6	2.6	5.6	1.5	2.1	3.0
Friends of relatives	4.6	4.0	4.6	1.6	4.6	4.4
Own friends	12.4	13.5	11.4	4.4	18.7	12.9
Laborers	47.8	43.8	42.0	43.9	53.1	46.9
Relatives	22.1	22.8	24.9	14.7	23.4	22.5
Friends of relatives	3.1	2.7	0.7	2.9	3.9	2.8
Own friends	22.6	18.3	16.4	26.3	25.8	21.6
No. of workers	2349	603	614	159	531	4249

[a] This does not represent all of the contacts inasmuch as only one category was checked for each respondent. This was done by counting a response at the highest possible row in the table; that is, supervisors took precedence over laborers and relatives over non-relatives in the tabulation. It is assumed that this system would follow the worker's own practice in using "influence" in getting his job.

TABLE XXVII

ASSISTANCE GIVEN TO WORKERS WITH CONTACTS IN
COMPANY AT HIRING TIME, BY FACTORY
(Per Cent)

Nature of Assistance	Textile	Paper	Engine	Biscuit	Rubber	All Factories
Recommended	51.2	75.5	58.4	43.6	64.9	57.3
Informed of job only	16.4	6.7	8.0	27.3	11.6	13.5
Other help	15.5	10.1	11.0	10.1	12.1	13.5
No help	16.9	7.7	20.7	19.0	9.8	15.2
No information	——	——	1.9	——	1.6	0.5
No. of cases	1577	391	390	82	417	2857

cases (57.7 per cent) this included recommending him to his employer. The central importance of the extended kin group in the network of influence may be seen by adding together relatives and acquaintances who were known through relatives. This makes up 48.4 per cent of all contacts within the factory at hiring time. It is also interesting to note that the bulk of these useful contacts in all of the factories were below the supervisory level.

To summarize, then, the use of formal channels for securing a job still runs a poor second to influence, and the most common form of influence is to use a friend at court, preferably a kinsman. The process works fairly simply: most of the factories inform their own employees when they are in need of workers and they in turn recruit from among their friends and relatives.

Worker's Commitment

One can find in the literature various descriptions of Indian factory workers which will place them at all points along a continuum of commitment to their factory. Authors' opinions vary considerably: at one extreme are those who emphasize the continuing "village nexus" in which the workers are still presumed to be involved and which inhibits their transformation into an urban industrial proletariat; at the other extreme are those who would argue that the factory worker is, if not over-committed, at least less flexible than he should be. Those who emphasize the village nexus are usually either writing at a high level of generalization about India, are speaking of an earlier period of time, or are writing quasi-metaphorically, and use India as a presumed illustration of what is taken to be a general relationship between economic development and commitment of the labor force.[9]

[9] Many examples of this could be cited, but a few typical ones should suffice. See, for instance, Philip M. Hauser (ed.), *Urbanization in Asia and the Far East*, Calcutta: UNESCO (1957), pp. 181-183;

In some of the more specialized or more recent discussions of current Indian factory labor, the workers are placed a little further along the continuum. Charles Myers[10] speaks of the "partial commitment" of the Indian factory workers, viewing them as pushed out of the village by shrinking economic opportunities, but nonetheless with some continuing ties with the village reinforced by a repellent push from the cities.[11] He sees the resultant partial commitment as expressing itself in high absenteeism, but not in high turnover. Some evidence for the continuity of village ties is found in Prabhu's sample survey of Bombay textile workers,[12] in which about three-fourths of the workers visited their villages at least once a year; most of them only once a year. At the same time, he notes: "It is quite apparent that an overwhelming majority of migrants are generally content with their job situation or are adjusting themselves to their work in the mills and factories."[13] Myers puts this position of partial commitment most succinctly: "In a sense, these Indian workers want to have their cake and eat it too: they are partially committed to factory jobs in that they regard

---

or O. H. K. Spate, *India and Pakistan, A General and Regional Geography*, New York: E. P. Dutton & Co., Inc. (1954), pp. 279-80; or W. Norman Brown, *The United States and India and Pakistan*, Cambridge: Harvard University Press (1953), p. 233; or Oscar Ornati, *Jobs and Workers in India*, Ithaca, N.Y.: Cornell University Press (1955).

[10] Charles A. Myers, *Labor Problems in the Industrialization of India*, Cambridge: Harvard University Press, 1958, Ch. III.

[11] On this point, see also Bert F. Hoselitz, "The City, The Factory and Economic Growth," *The American Economic Review*, 45:166-184 (May 1955).

[12] P. N. Prabhu, "Bombay: A Study of the Social Effects of Urbanization on Industrial Workers Migrating from Rural Areas to the City of Bombay," in *The Social Implications of Industrialization and Urbanization: Five Studies in Asia*, Calcutta: UNESCO (1956), pp. 49-106.

[13] *Ibid.*, p. 63.

them as more or less permanent which can be interrupted (but not lost) by periodic visits to the village."[14]

Other writers would put somewhat less emphasis upon the continuing village ties, moving the workers even further along the commitment continuum. Morris D. Morris' trenchant critique of Prabhu speaks of "The myth of 'Paradise Lost' "[15] and the "mystique of urban horrors" to urge that factory workers who migrate from the rural areas are not so unhappy as they are often depicted. Sometimes a high level of commitment is described as a new phenomenon in India, consequent upon the development of an urban industrial proletariat in recent decades.[16] Others argue that even in earlier periods, the difficulty of breaking village ties and of adjustment to the factory environment has been exaggerated. In another article, Morris writes:

"Historical evidence indicates that the transformation of a rural, traditionally organized population into a committed industrial labor force has not been socially difficult in India. The desperate poverty of the countryside made available a large labor supply that was eager to move into industry as opportunity appeared. Once employed in the factories, the workers on the whole rather readily adjusted to the disciplinary requirement of mechanized industry."[17]

Another step in the journey along the commitment continuum is taken by those who argue that the fundamental problem is not worker commitment but management commitment: most of the remaining casualization of the

[14] Myers, op.cit., p. 45.
[15] The Economic Weekly, July 6, 1957, pp. 857-62.
[16] See, for instance, Labour Investigation Committee, Main Report, Government of India (1946); or Bert F. Hoselitz, "The Market Matrix," in Moore and Feldman, op.cit., p. 224.
[17] Morris D. Morris, "The Labor Market in India," in Moore and Feldman, op.cit., p. 199.

workforce is the result of owners', not workers', reluctance to make the tie binding.[18]

In part, the disagreements reflected by these different positions are the result of different levels of generalization, and in part of taking different sub-sets of data from a wide variety of situations and times in India. The data of the present study cannot resolve the debate about which of the various positions most adequately describes the modal worker or the majority of Indian workers, since they, too, refer to only one situation and one point in time. Moreover, some of the data necessary to resolve the theoretical debate even for the workers in the Poona factories were not collected or did not prove to be of sufficient accuracy to be reported. For instance, we have no data on absenteeism, or on internalization of work rules, nor do any of the data deal directly with currently active village ties. Nevertheless, some of our data do reflect upon crucial parts of the argument, and they do have a special, perhaps specious, advantage in assessing the workers' allegiance to the village and their commitment to the factory: we asked them.

To examine the relevance of these data to commitment theory, let us utilize Moore and Feldman's "stages of commitment."

[18] See Morris D. Morris, "The Supply of Labour to the Bombay Cotton Textile Industry, 1854-1951," *The Indian Economic Journal*, October 1953, pp. 151-152; Daniel Thorner, "Casual Employment of a Factory Labour Force, 1851-1939," *The Economic Weekly Annual*, January 1957, pp. 121-124; Ralph C. James, "Labor Mobility, Unemployment, and Economic Change: An Indian Case," *The Journal of Political Economy*, December 1957, pp. 545-559; and Ralph C. James, "The Casual Labor Problem in Indian Manufacturing," *The Quarterly Journal of Economics*, February 1960, pp. 100-116.

The only sources I have heard referring to overcommitment have been employers who have difficulty discharging inefficient employees. They have been known to wish their employees' commitment were a little less firm.

"The committed worker has severed his connection with the land and with his tribal background. He is fully urbanized and never expects to leave industrial life. His family is permanently resident in an urban area, and it is not unusual for the wife also to enter the labor market. In fact, one good test of the degree of commitment of a labor force is the percentage of it comprised by women. An uncommitted or semicommitted labor force is predominantly male. The uncommitted worker depends for his security on his employer and on the state, not his tribe. His way of life is industrial.

"The overcommitted worker is committed not only to industrial life but also to his particular occupation or his particular employer by training, by seniority rules, and by pension and welfare programs. He is not just a member of a permanent labor force, but of a small and closely prescribed segment of it. He is back in the closed circle of the 'tribe,' subject again to custom and to duty to the group."[19]

To examine the first set of characteristics indicating the degree of a worker's commitment, we tried to determine if the worker has severed his connection with the land and become fully urbanized, and does he ever expect to leave industrial life. While we did not explore current village ties, we did ask the workers whether they would like to retire to a village if they had accumulated enough money to live on. In view of the fact that some 30 per cent of the workers were born and raised in Poona, and an undetermined proportion of migrants had come from other urban rather than rural areas, it was somewhat surprising to find that 30.8 per cent (40.8 in the textile mill) of the workers indicated that they would like to round out their lives in a village. This would seem to put a fair proportion of the

[19] Moore and Feldman, op.cit., pp. 351-352.

workers at the lower end of the commitment continuum.

The second characteristic emphasized by Moore and Feldman is the proportion of females among the factory workers. The scarcity of women in these five factories in both absolute terms and vis-à-vis the Poona labor force as a whole also seems to place these workers at the lower end of the commitment scale.

Other data we collected, however, seem to place the workers in the committed, or perhaps the over-committed category. Table XXVIII shows the proportion of workers who gave affirmative responses to questions about whether if they were laid off they would seek another job in a factory, in the same occupation as the one they were currently practicing, and whether they would restrict their search to Poona.[20]

TABLE XXVIII

PER CENT OF ALL WORKERS COMMITTED TO FACTORY, OCCUPATION AND CITY, BY FACTORY

Type of Attachment	Textile	Paper	Engine	Biscuit	Rubber	All Factories
Factory	73.4	64.7	89.8	77.5	85.9	76.2
Occupation	50.8	31.1	51.1	34.4	39.6	46.0
City (Poona)	1.8	4.5	5.5	12.6	11.2	4.3

If we view commitment as the intention to try to remain in factory employment, more than three-fourths of the workers are committed. If we take Moore and Feldman's notion of occupational commitment as over-commitment, almost half the workers show this degree of commitment.

[20] The hypothetical lay-off was put into the question so the workers' specific reactions to their *present* factory would not be confounded with their general commitment to factory work. Their attitudes toward their present factory will be examined in Chapter V.

The comparatively low proportion of workers who would insist on working in Poona shows how much stronger the employment commitment is than the residential commitment.

Thus, if we follow the Moore and Feldman conception of "stages of commitment," even this small sample of factory workers spreads across the continuum. We can, I believe, clarify the evidence somewhat by looking more closely at the data already given. In the first place, answers to the retirement question are probably neither realistic statements of actual intentions nor a true index of the workers' continuing village ties. By linking the question to retirement and an ample income we probably evoked in some of the workers utopian phantasies, idyllic notions of peace and tranquility with which sentimental urbanites imbue the countryside the world over. As Prabhu, commenting on his own data, puts it, "Studied in the totality of the situation we find that the responses eulogizing everything rural is more a sentimental feeling than a result of the inconveniences and difficulties met with in the city."[21]

The low proportion of women in the factories is a more obstinate fact, but in India, at least, I suspect that Moore and Feldman are wrong in associating this phenomenon with low commitment. The proportion of women in the workforce is not entirely, or even primarily, a choice of the women or their families. Even with an abundant supply of women willing to work, it is up to the employer to hire them. In fact, in earlier decades, the evidence indicates that the proportion of women in the factory labor force was relatively high at the turn of the century and that for a

[21] Prabhu, op.cit., p. 87.

few decades they were replacing male workers.[22] The employment of female workers dropped sharply after the introduction of laws regulating the conditions under which women could work and adding special welfare provisions for female employees. There is little evidence of scarcity of female labor if the jobs were available, and particularly if their pay were equal to that of males.

The notion that occupational commitment represents over-commitment is probably put too baldly here even for Moore and Feldman. What they must mean is the equivalent to what was meant by Charles Wilson's ill-fated distinction between workers who were like watch dogs as against those who were like bird dogs. The former, equivalent to Moore and Feldman's over-committed workers, clung to a place and occupation or a particular plant when his economic advantage should have made him like the bird dog, more sensitive to better opportunities elsewhere. We have no data on this hypothetical canine analogy from our workers.

The evidence of Table XXVIII seems a realistic enough measure of what a more limited meaning of commitment might imply, and thus the workers might best be placed well along the commitment continuum. When we look at the individual factories, we see that the workers in all seem to have a fairly high commitment. As might be expected, Types B and C, whose workers have occupational titles and machine skills that are easily transferable to many other units, show the highest degree of occupational commitment. The least commitment to the city was among the textile workers who, as we pointed out earlier, had already worked in most of the other mills in Bombay state.

[22] Pravakar Sen, "Supply of Industrial Labour in India, 1892-1943," *The Economic Weekly*, May 26, 1956, p. 610.

There were, of course, varying degrees of intensity in each type of commitment mentioned above. In each factory, however, there were some (18.3 per cent) who stated that they would definitely not seek another job in the factory. The older factories—textile and paper—had the highest proportions, with 22.2 and 23.9 per cent respectively, the two newest factories—engine and rubber—the fewest, with 7.8 and 7.1 per cent respectively, and the slightly older biscuit factory 17.7. This ranking of factories suggested the hypothesis that the desire to leave the factory increased with age or, more properly, the younger generation was more committed to the factory than the older generation of workers. Whether or not the current younger generation will become more disenchanted as they get older cannot be seen from a cross-sectional survey. To explore this hypothesis, age, length of time in the labor force, and length of time in factory employment were all tested for their association with desire to seek other than factory employment if there was a retrenchment. All associations were positive and significant in each factory.

There are several other factors which one might expect would be correlated with commitment to the factory. One would have anticipated that those who had served in other factories as well as the present one would be less likely to want to leave factory employment, but there was no clear relationship of this kind. One might have expected that the more skilled, the higher paid, would be more committed, but this does not appear to be so. Nor are the educated more eager to leave the factory. Nor does the size of the worker's family seem to affect it one way or the other.

The statistical manifestation of workers' commitment to a single factory is low turnover rates. Since this survey was taken at a single point in time, serial data on turnover rates cannot be given. Those who have left the factories are precisely those who will not be caught in a sample taken from current employee rolls. Nor do many companies keep records in a form which would permit ready and accurate estimation of turnover. What the questionnaires do give us is seniority as a record of survival from past turnover. Table XXIX indicates the year of joining the present factory and the median seniority of all workers by factory.

TABLE XXIX

YEAR FIRST EMPLOYED IN PRESENT FACTORY
FOR ALL WORKERS, BY FACTORY

Year Hired	Textile	Paper	Engine	Biscuit	Rubber
Before 1927	1.1	7.4	—	—	—
1927-31	3.6	6.9	—	1.6	—
1932-36	5.4	9.2	—	4.4	—
1937-41	11.9	14.3	—	2.9	—
1942-46	24.0	25.4	0.3	40.0	8.0
1947-51	31.8	16.7	49.9	27.6	15.9
1952	5.1	0.8	3.2	2.3	4.9
1953	1.7	8.0	8.7	1.6	4.9
1954	2.4	6.4	12.5	0.8	9.7
1955	3.6	3.2	16.5	1.5	37.1
1956	9.4	1.6	8.9	17.2	19.5
Number	2342	603	614	159	531
Median seniority	9.4	14.6	5.0	8.1	1.8

It will be recalled that the textile and paper mills have been in operation since the turn of the century, so the upper limits of seniority are therefore not fixed by the newness of the factory as they are in the post-World War II engine and rubber factories and the biscuit factory of the 1930's. The relatively high median seniority (9.4 and 14.6 years respectively), and the fact that only about one-fifth of the workers in each company have been employed there for less than five years, indicate a fairly substantial stability of the workforce.

Like turnover, however, seniority distribution cannot be directly translated into indices of "commitment." While it is true that an old company with an average seniority of about a year might indicate low commitment, and a mean seniority of thirty years might indicate a high commitment, values in between these extremes reflect at least such gross variables as fluctuations in the total number of workers, as well as such immeasurables as a general company policy of short-term employment to discourage the growth of claims for job security and fringe benefits. We shall return to this point shortly.

TABLE XXX

TOTAL NUMBER OF WORKERS, BY FACTORY, BY YEAR

Year	Textile	Paper	Engine	Biscuit	Rubber
1950	1700	493	273	216	207
1951	—	—	376	208	248
1952	—	—	349	189	307
1953	—	—	379	125	252
1954	1718	517	415	112	295
1955	1725	543	481	104	375
1956	2173	536	539	129	473

Recent fluctuations in the total workforces of the five factories are given in Table XXX. It will be noted that the two newest factories, the engine and rubber factories, have been gradually expanding, each with one over-production crisis that resulted in a reduction of the workforce —1952 in the engine factory and 1953 in the rubber factory. The biscuit factory has been gradually reducing the number of employees while increasing its output by the introduction of automatic equipment, with one major drop in the number of employees in the transfer of operations to a new, partially automated factory in 1952. The paper mill has been relatively stable throughout its recent history. The textile mill was also stable until the introduction of a third shift in 1956.

Now, if we look again at the comparative seniority figures in Table XXIX, we will see that many of the differentials are largely explainable in terms of the idiosyncratic fluctuations in the total number of workers in each factory. The highly stable paper factory has the highest average seniority. The profile and average seniority in the textile mill would be much the same as in the paper mill except for sudden spurts right after the war and in 1956. The biscuit factory has almost cut its workforce in half, so that in spite of its greater life span as compared with the engine factory, its median seniority is not much higher. The engine factory, in existence for only ten years, nevertheless has a median seniority of five years, in spite of almost doubling its workforce since 1950. This indicates there is already a fairly high degree of commitment on the part of its workers. The rubber factory, with its low median seniority, has been the least stable of all. Although it almost doubled the total number of workers on the company rolls since 1950, it had a severe business shock accompanied by layoffs in 1953, and almost two-thirds of its workers were hired in the most recent three years.

The general conclusion to be drawn from this comparison, then, is that the seniority structure of the workforce is more a result of the vagaries of company history than of any lack of commitment to the job upon the part of labor. In fact, so clear is this general relationship that it puts severe limitations upon the usefulness of talking exclusively about worker commitment when one is concerned with the decasualization of a labor force without, at the same time, speaking of employer commitment.

One can, in fact, raise a question as to the usefulness of the concept of commitment to describe the relevant variables in the factory labor market situation in India. Myers' retreat to the notion of "partial commitment" seems to be an attempt to preserve the concept in the face of contradictory evidence. Since our own data would tend to place the workers at several points along the hypothetical commitment continuum and point to the determinative effect of market conditions beyond the individual worker's control, it seems better to return to an earlier set of terms to illuminate the findings. It will be recalled that in the Introduction we characterized a set of broad changes which were presumed to flow from industrialization and to mark the evolution away from traditional, folk societies to modern, mass societies. One of these was the transformation originally characterized by Sir Henry Maine as a change from societies based on status to those based on contract.[23] Traditional India, of course, is almost a prototype of the status-based society. Within the village, the caste system or some variation of the patron-client relationship, usually called the *Jajmani* system, assigns to specific families the right to perform and be rewarded for certain economic tasks. The family acquires a property right in a job and a clientele, and this right is in varying degrees heritable, mortgageable, and transferable. These job assignments both arise out of status in that the active pursuits tend to be the closed preserve of members of castes whose tradi-

[23] Sir Henry Maine, *Ancient Law*, ed. by Sir Frederick Pollock, New York: Henry Holt and Company, 1906.

tional occupations they are,[24] and give status in that the worker may derive prestige from the standing of his patron. The interlinking of an occupation and status resides in the fact of the job, not the quality of its performance. To be sure, the quality of performance must be sufficiently high not to violate relatively loose customary standards, but above that minimal level, for most artisans superior performance is accompanied by little elasticity in rewards other than personal esteem. The termination of the reciprocal relationships between patron and worker is by no means entirely in the hands of the patron, and he may find himself subject to a general caste boycott if he seeks to dissolve a long-term relationship.[25]

The carry-over of this general notion of reciprocal obligation between *jajman* and *purjan* into the factory employer-employee is relatively easy. The attention to the workers' property rights in the factory job is evident in the elaborate regulations concerning dismissal and the difficulty factories have in firing a permanent worker merely on the grounds of inefficiency. Both the day-to-day pressure of the union and the threat of a suit in the labor court act as a margin of safety for the property rights of the worker. The workers' right to compensation in case of layoffs further symbolizes the perquisites of status. At the same time, much of the "indiscipline" and low productivity which Myers refers to as partial commitment, and what the management often takes as an inevitable condition, derive from these same set of interpersonal norms. At the same time,

---

[24] For a discussion of this particular point, see E. R. Leach (ed.), *Aspects of Caste in South India, Ceylon and Northwest Pakistan,* Cambridge University Press, 1960, pp. 6 ff. A more general discussion may be found in the classic W. Wiser, *The Hindu Jajmani System.*

[25] I am speaking, of course, of artisan and service relationships, not agricultural tenants or landless laborers.

the expectation on the part of the worker is that his status as a worker, so long as he displays proper deference behavior to the owner, entitles him to various perquisites and special favors from the owner or his representative.[26]

The general point is not, then, that the workers are still oriented to a specific village, but to a village-based set of inter-personal relational norms which are infused throughout the traditional society and are carried over into the factory. This outlook explains in part the general lack of anxiety about the job market which our data showed. It may also explain why none of the factors such as education or skill level, which, on the basis of their genuine relationship to a worker's chances in the job market, we would have expected to reflect differences in the worker's assessment of his chances of success if forced to seek another job, did in fact correlate with variations in the workers' sense of security. This attitudinal carry-over operates in a market where the seeking of the status of jobholder still uses traditional mechanisms based upon the kin network and the use of "influence." It might also be added that enhanced workers' rights in their jobs is in accord with the concern of the welfare state for bolstering individual as against corporate economic advantage.

The net result of this carry-over of norms for the worker is to increase his security. In earlier periods, this was offset by labor hiring practices such as the system of hiring through contractors or jobbers who sometimes had an economic stake in high turnover. Since such practices are now almost obsolete, the status of factory jobholder tends to be a more durable property. From the viewpoint of the

[26] Cf. N. R. Sheth, "An Indian Factory—Aspects of its Social Framework," *Journal of M. S. University of Baroda*, 9:47-66 (March 1960).

management, however, this represents a curtailment of their ability to discipline, weed out, or reduce their workforce, and the companies have responded by making the status of jobholder a little more difficult to come by. This is done by creating a set of employees who work for the company but enjoy somewhat less than full status in it.

COMPANIES' COMMITMENT TO WORKERS

A common feature of the factory system in India is the retention of a part of the workforce in a "temporary" status, a term which applies not so much to time as to whether or not a worker holds full title to a job specified as part of the regular complement of workers for the factory. The job complement for a factory may be fixed either by a collective bargaining agreement between company and the union(s) or by an award emerging out of the governmental machinery for resolving labor disputes.[27] Such an award may refer either to an individual factory or, as in the case of textiles, to an entire industry, and ordinarily it will specify the ratio of men to machines, the skill categories and wage systems attributable to each type of work, various "fringe benefits" and the conditions under which they must be provided, and sometimes the amenities necessary to make working conditions tolerable. Workers who fill out the job complements are referred to as permanent employees and are entitled to such benefits as compensation when work is not available, a specified number of days of sick, annual, and casual leave during which the worker must be paid, commissary privileges where one exists, annual bonuses, provident fund membership, and whatever other contractual or legal rights accrue to workers. A company may extend any or all of these benefits to its tem-

[27] An example of a settlement is given in Appendix E.

porary workers, but it need not. Moreover, in the case of permanent workers, not only must a company find daily work no matter what the short-run market demand for its product, but discharge of such employees is almost always attended by trouble for the management. Much of the discussion about commitment of the labor force must sound ironic to employers who have been known to wish that some of their employees were a little less committed.

The job complement system tied to the workers' notions about property rights in a job has the effect of making the workforce in any factory inelastic. From the viewpoint of management it limits the ability of the company to respond to fluctuations in demand by expanding or contracting its labor force. The complex historical origins of the systems of less-than-permanent employment need not concern us here. In addition to providing for an apprenticeship and training period, their present functions are to preserve the company's flexibility in total labor supply and to limit the number of workers with contractually enforceable demands. Most factories retain an elastic supply of workers outside the job complement on a "temporary" basis. The workforce with less than permanent status in each factory varies from ten to twenty per cent as Table XXXI indicates.

The margin of workers at less than permanent status is maintained in these factories in two administrative categories—*badli* and temporary workers.

The two older factories, the textile and paper mills, use a *badli* system under which a registered group of workers present themselves each day at the factory gate to be used as substitutes for the absentees. *Badli* workers are arranged on the list by seniority. Those highest on the list are almost certain to get some work each day, while others work less often. It is also assumed that openings in the

TABLE XXXI

NUMBER AND PER CENT OF ALL WORKERS WITH
NON-PERMANENT STATUS, BY FACTORY

Factory	No. in Sample	No. in Factory	Per Cent of Workforce
Textile	32	427	18.2[a]
Paper	18	87	14.4
Engine	17	86	14.0
Biscuit	20	26	16.6
Rubber	13	57	10.7
All factories	100	683	16.0

[a] In cotton textile mills in Bombay City, the per cent of *badlis* in the mills varied between 15.1 and 19.8 during the years 1946-55. Ralph C. James, "Labor Mobility, Unemployment and Economic Change: An Indian Case," *The Journal of Political Economy*, December 1959, p. 553.

TABLE XXXII

PER CENT BADLI AND TEMPORARY AMONG
NON-PERMANENT WORKERS, BY FACTORY

Factory	Badli	Temporary	Number Non-Permanent
Textile	51.5	48.5	427
Paper	100.0	—	87
Engine	—	100.0	86
Biscuit	—	100.0	26
Rubber	—	100.0	57
All factories	44.9	55.1	683

permanent complement will be filled from the *badli* lists if the requisite skills can be found there.

The difference between *badli* and temporary workers may be seen most clearly in the textile mill, where both are employed. As distinct from the *badli* workers who are hired anew each day, in the textile mill there are three types of temporary workers. The first type performs the same kind of job as the permanent workers but the job complement has not been formally fixed. When the company expanded to three shifts and when it brought in a new type of loom in one weaving shed, it awaited the establishment of a new complement by an Industrial Tribunal before the jobs were given permanent status. At the time of the study, the tri-partite negotiations (management-labor-government) had not been completed and were expected to take many more months. In the meantime, workers who were filling the new jobs were retained in temporary status even though their pay and perquisites were *de facto* the same as those of workers with permanent status. A second type of temporary worker is the newcomer who fills a spot in the complement but serves an initial probationary period. A third category of temporary worker is one who is employed for a job which the company knows will last for a brief period of time and then will be discontinued. Construction workers are often hired in this way.

By way of contrast, none of the other factories employs both temporary and *badli* workers. The paper mill calls all of its non-permanent workers *badlis*, but they form a regular pool of casual laborers who are given some kind of work to do almost every day, even if a task has to be created for them. None of the newer factories uses the term *badli*, but each carries a numerically equivalent group of workers in temporary status, mostly under the apprentice and the short-term job systems.

Perhaps more indicative of the use which the individual factory makes of workers in this non-permanent labor pool is the consistency with which the workers are employed. In all but the textile mill, the vast majority of the non-permanent employees reported that they worked almost

every day during the six months preceding the interview.
The standard work month is 26 days. The following table
indicates the average number of days worked per month
during the preceding six months, as recalled by the worker,
and the mean range between the highest and lowest number of work days and wages. The mean range is computed
by taking the difference between the highest and lowest
number of days worked, or wage, in the previous six
months for each worker, summing these and dividing by
the number of non-permanent workers.

TABLE XXXIII

MEAN AND RANGE OF DAYS WORKED PER MONTH AND WAGES
DURING PREVIOUS SIX MONTHS, BY FACTORY

Factory	No. Days Worked		Rs. Wages	
	Mean	Range	Mean	Range
Textile	18.4	9.7	60.3	27.3
Paper	24.3	2.5	72.5	5.5
Engine	24.2	5.3	71.2	17.1
Biscuit	24.8	2.1	62.5	8.1
Rubber	25.6	2.4	52.1	1.8
All factories	20.7	6.8	62.7	17.2

It is clear that the textile mill is in fact using its non-
permanent workers for short-term fluctuations in demand
for labor, while the other companies utilize their non-permanent workers almost as fully as their permanent workers.
With the normal work month at 26 days, only the textile
mill workers depart very far from this full work schedule.
This is also reflected in the narrow range of wage fluctuations in most companies. The high range in the engine
factory was caused by a few temporary workers who
worked only about half the time in one or two months

while most workers were fully employed. In the four companies other than the textile mill, more than half of the non-permanent workers were employed every working day during the preceding six months.

The current operation of the historic *badli* system in the textile mill alone is understandable if we look again at our production system typology. In the Type A systems, substitutions for absentees must also be made, but the skill levels are low enough to allow easy transfer of relatively unskilled workers who can be kept in a temporary standing and sent from one job to another as they are needed. If the job is one of the more responsible positions in the gang operation, one of the remaining lower echelon members of the gang fills in. While the paper mill calls its system a *badli* system, it is very different from that in the Type B textile mill, where *badlis* lists are made up by specific skills and the substitutes fill in at fairly advanced skill levels. This is possible precisely because these machine-tending skills are individual—that is to say, if a worker is not there so many machines will not operate—but also interchangeable—that is to say, one spinner or one doffer boy can easily exchange with another one. While the employees in the Type C engine factory have a high degree of skill, individual workers are much less interchangeable without some special orientation to the task at hand, to which the worker must bring some creative skill, no matter how minimal. In the factory, then, temporary workers cannot easily fill in at the skilled worker level and are in fact either apprentices at the bottom, construction workers, or a surplus labor pool in each department.

Most, but not all, the non-permanent workers are employed in jobs in the lowest skill categories. The textile mill, with its elaborate *badli* system, and the engine factory, with an on-the-job training program, spread the temporary workers over their skill range. Table XXXIV gives the percentage of non-permanent workers employed at semi-skilled or skilled levels within each factory. However, in all factories, their average wage is equivalent to or less than that paid to the least skilled workers. The mean wage for all laborers in all factories is Rs. 84.1. For non-permanent workers it is Rs. 62.7, or slightly over the standard wage (Rs. 60) for a worker without any skills at all.

TABLE XXXIV

Per Cent of Non-Permanent Workers
Employed at Unskilled Jobs

Factory	Per Cent
Textile	56.2
Paper	88.9
Engine	70.6
Biscuit	95.0
Rubber	69.3
All factories	66.0

From the viewpoint of the worker, the policy of the companies of retaining a portion of the workforce in non-permanent status means that he will normally serve a probationary period in a temporary or *badli* status prior to his gaining title to a job in a regular complement. In most factories the majority of workers have been through a probationary period. Table XXXV gives the prevalence and the average duration of this period.

It will be readily seen that in all factories except the paper factory, 80 to 90 per cent of all workers at all grades have spent some time in a non-permanent status, and on the average the probation period was between two and three

TABLE XXXV

PERMANENT WORKERS REPORTING PREVIOUS
TEMPORARY STATUS, BY FACTORY

Factory	Per Cent of Workers	Median Duration Months	Per Cent Over 1 Year	No. of Permanent Workers in Factory	No. of Permanent Workers in Sample
Textile	86.2	2.2	5.2	1915	219
Paper	34.8	—	5.1	516	136
Engine	81.8	2.5	1.2	528	133
Biscuit	85.4	5.5	19.9	123	108
Rubber	92.4	2.8	7.8	474	125
All factories	78.9	2.0	5.5	3556	721

months. The biscuit factory, the smallest of the concerns, seems to have retained its workers in temporary status longest. Almost 20 per cent of its workers served more than a year without permanent appointment, with a median period of five and one-half months. The paper factory, which used the probation period the least, nevertheless kept 5 per cent of its permanent workers as *badlis* for over a year.

The figures in the table above, of course, cover a generation of company history and include only the survivors of the probation period who actually became permanent workers. It is interesting to compare their experience with the experience and expectations of workers who are currently in a non-permanent status.

Comparing Table XXXVI, which gives the seniority of workers currently in non-permanent status, with the duration of that status for currently permanent workers given in Table XXXV, we see that the use of non-permanent workers has changed with time. The two factories (biscuit and rubber) that had the record of longest probation periods in

RECRUITMENT AND COMMITMENT

TABLE XXXVI

SENIORITY OF WORKERS CURRENTLY
IN NON-PERMANENT STATUS

Factory	Median Months	Per Cent Over 1 Year
Textile	16.8	55.0
Paper	39.4	94.4
Engine	12.0	54.9
Biscuit	6.3	5.0
Rubber	6.0	—
All factories	17.7	53.5

the past had the highest turnover of temporary workers at the time of the study, and the other three kept their workers in non-permanent status much longer at the time of the study. The paper company is the most striking. It will be recalled that only about 35 per cent of their workers experienced non-permanent status, while 94 per cent of their *badlis* have more than a year's seniority, with a median of 39 months. It is impossible to make precise time comparisons because of the departure from the factories of an undetermined number of temporary workers at different periods in the past, but it does appear that the average time spent in non-permanent status is increasing in all the factories, and that the two older companies using the *badli* system have a non-permanent labor pool that is tending to become stabilized. It is true that the non-permanent workers are still young—their median age is 22.2 years as compared with the general average of 32.4—but even at this early age about 40 per cent of them have already worked in another factory before coming to their present employment, so they are not all new to the factory labor force. It remains to be seen whether the path to permanent employment will be as easy for them as it was for

102

their predecessors. It is clear that they do want and expect to become permanent. Only 6 per cent of the non-permanent workers indicated that they did not want to become permanent workers, and an additional 12.7 per cent thought they would never reach that status. About 35 per cent thought they would make it within the year.

One of the oldest criticisms of the system of employing workers on a non-permanent basis is that it permits the daily operation of favoritism by minor supervisory personnel. This no longer operates in its pure form since even *badli* lists are kept in strict seniority order, but a sizable proportion of the non-permanent workers reported that it still operates in the assignment of specific jobs. The non-permanent workers were asked to state whether they believed there was any favoritism (vashilebājī) operating in the assignment of jobs. Table XXXVII indicates the number who replied yes to this question.

TABLE XXXVII

NON-PERMANENT WORKERS REPORTING FAVORITISM
IN JOB ASSIGNMENT, BY FACTORY

Factory	Number Yes Sample	Total Non-Permanent Sample
Textile	15	32
Paper	14	18
Engine	9	17
Biscuit	2	20
Rubber	4	12
All factories	44	99

As a follow-up to this point, an open-end question, which asked those workers who reported favoritism to say how it worked, was included. All but three of them stated that knowing the head of a department was the key variable. It is interesting that only one worker, a Brahman who

103

worked in the paper factory, mentioned caste. He felt that his Brahman status was a handicap, not an asset.

The importance of influence in securing a job, discussed in a previous section, seems to pervade the day-to-day work assignments as well, and brings us back to our point that the transitional zone of temporary standing, which the companies set up to preserve some degree of flexibility in dealing with their workforce, is based on and supported by traditional attitudes about the role of status in determining property rights in a source of livelihood.

SUMMARY

By the time the workers reach their present factory employment, between one-fourth and one-third of the new employees had worked at similar jobs before, a little less than one-half had worked in factories before, and about two-thirds had been employed before. The range of experience was very wide, both in geographic spread and in the economic categories represented. As expected, the factories more active in socializing raw recruits were the Type A factories. The workers' experience in the job market had been relatively easy and they showed little evidence of insecurity. Influence, particularly through the kin network, as against the more formal mechanisms of job seeking, was still the primary basis of securing a job. Data on workers' commitment gave conflicting indications, and the simple notion of status and job rights was introduced. On the part of management, this resulted in a series of devices to hold about 20 per cent of the workforce in less than permanent status. The use of the classic form of the *badli* system was most characteristic of the Class B factory. The duration of the temporary status seemed to be increasing.

CHAPTER IV · INTERNAL STRUCTURE

▌▌▌▌ SO FAR, we have penetrated very little into the factories themselves. We have talked about the social characteristics of their workforces, of the amount and degree of experience that the workers bring to the factory, the ways in which they seek and gain entrance into the factory, and the temporary status through which they must pass until they reach full status in the factory. Once the worker has passed from non-permanent status into full property rights in his job, what manner of social organization does he enter and how does it affect his work career? How does our production system typology reflect itself in the internal structure of the factories? To elucidate further our typology, which will be of greater importance in this and the following chapter, let us call on another element of our general theme.

It will be recalled that in our introductory characterization of the literature on the impact of industrialization on traditional, agrarian societies, one of the presumed changes was the supplanting of primary group-organized production processes by a more complex division of labor, finer job specification, and the interdependence of separate economic roles.

All the factories of our sample do represent some departure from traditional primary group-organized production processes in that the family is no longer the basic unit of production. Of course, for many sections of the population in urban areas, the separation of work from the family had been accomplished long before the introduction of the factory, and such separation may be found today in many sections of society that are not engaged in factory employment. It is true, however, that factory employment makes

105

a more violent break between the family and work in that the factory walls prevent interaction between the earner and his family throughout the shift period, and there is no carry-over of work activities into the family life. The major contact between the two spheres of life are in the provision by the factory of support for the family, the demands for leave time to attend to family functions, and the use of the kin network in securing appointments. Occupational gradations within the factory, except perhaps for clerical, supervisory, or P & M divisions, have little transfer value for family prestige except as they are reflected in consumption. The general category "factory worker" is as fine a gradation in prestige ranking as is likely to have relevance for family standing in the community and, more important-ly, in one particular household's standing among other households in the extended family structure.

Aside from the insulation of the family from work, how-ever, the factories did differ in the extent to which their internal organization reflected the shift away from primary group organization. Type A, including three out of the five factories with their gang-organized machine tending, was still largely composed of primary group production units. The division of labor in these factories was relatively slight, job specifications were relatively crude, comprising some subdivision of the total job of care and feeding of a particu-lar machine. The interdependence of separate economic roles was relatively great within the gang, but inter-dependent among gangs only in the sense that in the pro-duction process materials flowed from one gang to another on their way through the sequence of machines. The super-visor was a gang-boss whose role was not unlike that of the eldest working male in a joint family work unit. The interactions within the factory were direct and face-to-face

106

within the gang and were often organic and semi-familial. The system would not have been hampered if the different gangs were in fact kin units supervised by their patres familias.

In the Type B factory, represented by the textile mill, complexity in the division of labor and fineness in job specification had gone to the extreme. Every one of the separate production tasks had a separate occupational name, and the work was subdivided into more than a hundred occupational titles. Intimate social relations among the workers were considered irrelevant, even detrimental to the production process, and friendships should in any event have been kept separate so that they did not interfere with the individual tending his machine or machines. The operation of the primary production processes, spinning and weaving, depended upon the proper role performance of the fitters, beam setters, beam carriers, doffer boys, and so on. It would appear that this sharp partitioning and interlocking of separate economic roles would form a fairly precise parallel to the caste system, and indeed the lack of vertical mobility among occupational titles would emphasize that parallel. There is, however, one necessary element of the village system of interlocked specific roles which is lacking. In the case of castes, the units in the division of labor are themselves primary groups: the families would comprise a caste. One of the interesting results of the Tavistock Institute's experiment in an Ahmedabad textile mill was that the regrouping of the workers into primary group units by mutual selection quickly raised productivity and satisfaction.[1] In Poona,

[1] A. F. Rice, *Productivity and Social Organization, The Ahmedabad Experiment,* London: Tavistock Publications, Ltd., 1958.

however, the textile mill was as far as possible from the primary group organization.

In the example of a Type C factory—the engine factory —the primary group had also given way to a division of labor on the basis of the functions of individuals, but the segmentation of occupational roles was not nearly so great nor so inflexible. The core of the workforce was made up of no more than half a dozen occupational titles, and each one had a skill gradation within it. With such a system, socialization to higher skill training is continually in process, so there is in fact some parallel to the guild-like apprenticeship of the urban artisans. Any group-like characteristics that do arise are therefore vertical rather than essentially flat as in the gang-machine tending factories. By and large, however, the production process is organized around the skilled performance of individuals, not interacting groups, and the appearance of "groups" on the factory floor is due to the geography of the plant, with all machines of a single type together under the control of a few supervisors. The high level of skill of the individual workers increases their personal responsibility and independence from detailed supervision and further heightens the decline of the group aspect. It should be said that throughout this discussion I do not mean to imply that the universal tendency toward the formation of cliques and friendship groups was not expressed in the Type B and C factories, but only that they were not reinforced by the organization of the productive process.

We see then, that the factory types do differ in the extent to which the primary group has been displaced from the production process, in the degree of complexity of the division of labor, and in the interdependence of separate economic roles. Let us see what consequences the production system typology has in the hierarchical ordering of the workforce.

HIERARCHICAL RANKING

Current Wages

Some clue to the over-all hierarchical structure may be gained from an examination of the frequency distribution of current wages for each factory.

The data which follow are based largely upon the workers' statements of their current wages. A check for the reliability of the information was made with payroll records in two companies and found sufficiently accurate to be used. The advantages of taking the workers' accounts are several. In the first place, the workers' and the company's reckoning of total wages is different. The worker reports his monthly take-home pay, which comprises the basic wage attached to the job he performs plus any seniority increments he has acquired and a "dearness allowance," a cost-of-living supplement to his basic wage. The companies in their reckoning of the wage bill average in other more occasional payments and various fringe benefits. For instance, in the engine factory, their account of average wages for P & M workers (workers other than clerks and supervisors) is shown in Table XXXVIII.

From the workers' own accounts the mean monthly wage in this factory for the equivalent group of workers would have been Rs. 93/1, an amount roughly equivalent to the basic wage and dearness allowance alone. While the company's account reflects the total wage bill, the workers' accounts reflects what they regularly have to spend. Other sums are treated by them as windfalls.

The other reason for using workers' accounts is that we will also be using data on their wage and occupational

TABLE XXXVIII

COMPANY STATEMENT SHOWING MEAN MONTHLY EARNINGS OF
P & M WORKERS IN THE ENGINE FACTORY IN 1956

	Rs/As
Basic Wage	57/2
Dearness Allowance	40/4
Attendance Prize	3/6
Production Bonus	58/12
Leave, Provident Fund, Insurance	16/1
Total	175/9

careers since they entered the current factory. These data are almost impossible to get from company records in most of the factories, where records are classified not by workers but by time period. For instance, the textile mill had records of workers' assignment to specific jobs entered on daily muster sheets. Conceivably the vicissitudes of occupants of a particular post in the job complement could be traced by comparing the daily muster sheets over a period of time, but even these data would be confusing in view of the daily adjustments in labor force distribution depending upon the type and amount of cloth or yarn being produced, and in view of the haphazard leave schedules and *badli* systems. There was no simple way of tracing precisely the work career of an individual. Even the tedious tracing of names was unrewarding in view of the great duplication of names, particularly in some castes. For the following accounts, then, workers' statements of their wages are used. In any event, inaccuracies of rounding and petty exaggerations did not radically affect the ranking of workers, which is what we are interested in primarily.

Table XXXIX and Graphs 1 to 5 give the percentage distribution of wage groups in each of the factories. Three

TABLE XXXIX

PER CENT OF PERMANENT P & M WORKERS IN EACH CURRENT
WAGE GROUP, BY FACTORY

Total Monthly Wage	Textile (N = 127)	Paper (N = 93)	Engine (N = 87)	Biscuit (N = 78)	Rubber (N = 90)
50-9	0.79	3.23	—	—	11.11
60-9	0.79	9.68	20.69	1.28	73.33
70-9	9.45	34.41	18.39	29.49	5.57
80-9	24.41	17.20	18.39	34.62	2.22
90-9	20.47	16.13	8.05	12.82	2.22
100-9	33.07	5.38	9.20	10.26	—
110-9	7.09	3.23	1.14	5.13	1.11
120-9	0.79	3.23	6.90	1.28	2.22
130-9	1.57	3.23	6.90	2.56	—
140-9	—	2.14	3.44	2.50	1.11
150 and over	1.57	2.14	6.90	—	1.11
Total	100.00	100.00	100.00	100.00	100.00
Mean	93.84	85.30	93.07	77.06	66.68
Median	95	80	82	72	60
	18.39	42.21	28.04	18.04	24.73*

* Without one case of Rs. 250, this would be 15.39, which is more representative of dispersion.

groups of workers are excluded from these tables because they would too radically distort the summary statistics—the temporary workers, the supervisors and clerks—so that the tables reflect only the wages of permanent P & M workers. From the Table and Graphs the general outline of the factory structures is quickly apparent. The mean wages in the textile mill and engine factory, Rs. 93.84 and Rs. 93.07, were considerably higher than those in the other three factories. This dichotomy, of course, coincides with our earlier typology distinguishing between the gang-organized, machine-tending production systems (Type A) in the paper, biscuit, and rubber factories on the one hand, and

111

GRAPHS 1 through 5: Percent of Permanent P & M Workers in each Current Wage Group

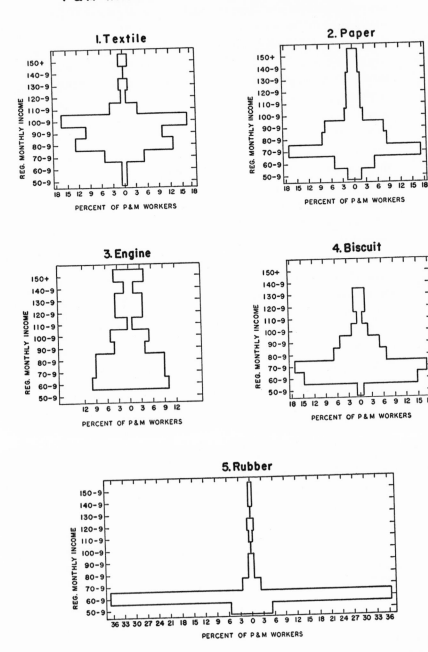

the lower man-to-machine ratio and higher degree of skills required in the textile and engine factories. The distinction between the skills required in the Type B textile mill, where one man tends to the repetitive operation of one or more machines without manipulating the machines' activities, and the Type C engine factory, where men use machines as tools and use their skills to direct them, was also reflected in the wage distribution. While the mean monthly wages were about the same in the two factories, the distribution of wages was very different. This difference is apparent both in the summary statistics at the bottom of the table and in the graphs. In the textile mill the mean and the median were about the same, and the dispersion as measured by the standard deviation was relatively low. This was a result of the heavy clustering of spinners and weavers in the middle of the distribution, which produced the diamond shaped outline in Graph 1 with its relatively thin superstructure of advanced skills and relatively small percentage of unskilled workers. The engine factory was basically of the pyramidal type, but it had a heavy column of highly skilled workers going up into the highest wage categories. In the table this shows up in the high standard deviation and in the great difference between the median and the mean, Rs. 93.07 and Rs. 82, respectively.

The three Type A factories had a large proportion of their workers at the lowest levels and approached the ideal typical slab form of organization. The most spectacular example is the rubber factory, where almost three-fourths of the P & M workers were receiving the wages of unskilled workers. This is a case of what might be called retarded growth. Because of the sometimes precarious financial position of the firm and the unwillingness of both the union and the government conciliators to threaten the company's survival by forcing a sudden increase in the wage load, the company continued to pay the vast majority of its workers a flat salary at the level of unskilled workers. A current industrial court dispute promised to produce a compromise between the two widely different plans submitted by the management and the union for expanding the wage hierarchy to fit the actual skill structure within the factory. But even with a new arbitration award, the basic structure is likely to resemble the slab model.

A comparison of the paper mill and the biscuit factory highlights another set of factors in the determination of the wage structure: the seniority of the workforce. Both companies utilized about the same level of skills in their manufacturing processes. Both are Type A. The difference between them is that the paper mill has been operating in its present form for more than a generation and hence its workers have high seniority. Since both factories have a system of giving periodic increments in wages even where the same task is being performed, with low turnover rates and a relatively stable total labor force, the average wage was higher in the older company. The longer the factory has been operating in the same fashion, the more likely it is that an increasing number of workers in relatively unskilled jobs will be paid higher wages. Accordingly, we find a higher mean wage in the paper mill, Rs. 85.30 compared with Rs. 77.06 in the biscuit factory, and a higher proportion of workers paid more than Rs. 110—14 per cent compared with 3.8 per cent in the biscuit factory.

The Occupational Ladder

So far we have been speaking of the hierarchical structure of the factories in terms of differences in total wages. For a number of reasons, however, we need a more refined classification of hierarchical position to compare accurately the occupational careers of workers in the five factories. While the current wage distribution for each company gives a useful picture of the actual wage structure, it is misleading if it is used as a measure of the skill or status structure in a factory. For one thing, the practice of paying dearness allowances (D.A.), a practice developed during World War II to meet a rapid increase in the cost of living without permanently inflating the wage bill, has grown to such proportions that in many cases differences in the D.A. alone are responsible for variations among the companies in wage levels. For instance, in the factory with the highest average wage, the textile factory, the D.A. was pegged to the cost of living index of nearby Sholapur and at the time of the study varied throughout the year from about Rs. 50 to Rs. 60 per month according to the season and the price of food grains. The factory with the second highest wage level, the engine factory, paid a D.A. of Rs. 1/6 per day to workers earning less than Rs. 2 per day in basic wages and Rs. 1/12 for those making more than Rs. 2. In the average month, this amounted to Rs. 38/8 per month at the lowest wage levels and Rs. 49 at the highest. The third ranking factory, the paper mill, paid 67 1/2 per cent of the Bombay Textile D.A.; the fourth, the biscuit factory, paid 66 2/3 of the same rate or about Rs. 40 per month. The lowest ranking factory, the rubber factory, paid a flat Rs. 35 per month.

Some of the D.A. were mildly progressive in that they increased slightly as the wage level increased. The engine factory rate given above is an example of this. However, the general effect of the D.A. system is to obscure wage differentials based upon skill levels or experience. For instance, for an unskilled worker in the textile factory who received the legal minimum of a rupee per day as a basic wage, the D.A. provided more than two-thirds of his total income. As a corollary to this situation, it may be remarked that the pecuniary motivation of a worker to rise in the job hierarchy is minimized when upward mobility is likely to bring him only a basic wage increase of, say, Rs. 5 and no increase in D.A.—that is, only about one-twentieth of his total wage and less than the amount that normal fluctuations of the D.A. might bring him in any given month. The flat rate system of D.A., whether based on cost of living or not, makes the gradations in basic wage rates a small part of the pay of the workers and decreases the gap between the skilled and unskilled workers in the factory.

The second factor which makes the current total wage distribution an unreliable guide to the skill and status structure of the factory is that in all factories except the textile mill an individual's basic wage depended upon his seniority. Pay scales were set in terms of a minimum rate and an annual increment up to a maximum level. For instance, the basic pay of the lowest skill grade in the biscuit factory was stated as follows: Rs. 26—As. 12—Rs. 32—Rs. 1—Rs. 40. This indicated that the worker who started at Rs. 26 per month basic wage received a 12 anna raise each of the first eight years of service until he reached Rs. 32 per month, and thereafter an increase of Rs. 1 for eight more years until he reached an upper limit of Rs. 40 so long as he remained in the same job. In general, the greater the seniority and the higher the skill grade, the larger the annual increment. The upper limit for one skill grade usually was higher than the starting wage for the next skill grade. For instance, in the biscuit factory, again, the lowest rank in the semi-skilled range started at Rs. 35 per month, which was Rs. 5 below the highest basic salary for the unskilled worker.

In addition to variable dearness allowances and seniority payments, idiosyncratic factors, such as a short-term scarcity of a certain skill or the particular year in which a worker was hired, may make one worker's current wage more than another for roughly the same work. These ad hoc wage fluctuations do not reflect either the company's or the worker's conceptions of occupational rankings.

To make a useful comparison of the hierarchical features of the different factories we must eliminate the distortions introduced by dearness allowances, seniority awards and idiosyncratic features. What we seek is a measure which is useful for five factories each manufacturing a different product, a measure which will rank occupations and not depend upon the attributes of the particular man who fills it or the peculiarities of the time when the job was filled. At this point it might be thought that it would be wise to seek some other means of occupational ranking, leaving wages aside entirely. There are, of course, general occupational classifications available, but most occupational classifications, when they do subdivide factory workers into distinct categories, ordinarily partition the workforce into industries first, and then make the occupational subdivisions within industries. In a two- or three-digital occupational code, the first one or two digits normally indicates the industry.[2] Moreover, few classifications make any attempt at ranking occupations. They are normally satisfied to provide a relatively exhaustive listing. The very few classifications that do rank occupations across industries use a rough-skilled, semi-skilled and unskilled trichotomy.

[2] This is true of the ILO's International Standard Classification of Occupations (ISCO), as well as the variant of that system developed by Indian Statistical Institute and called the National Standard Classification of Occupations.

Occupational dictionaries that make some such rating system have been drawn almost exclusively from Western economies, where the skill of the worker is considered the most important variable for ranking an occupation within the factory. This heavy emphasis upon the worker's skill in placing him within a hierarchy is an unreliable guide to occupational status rankings in Indian factories, where, while the terminology of skill is used to describe the various levels within the factory, many other variables are equally if not more heavily weighted than skill. Some evidence of the difference in values intrinsic to occupational rankings may be seen in a study conducted for the Ahmedabad Textile Industry Research Association by Kamla Chowdry and V. R. Trivedi.[3] In an attempt to rationalize wage differentials they asked twelve technicians with long experience in textile mills to rank the occupations in a mill and then independently to rate them on several criteria. The results were factor analyzed and the relative weights of the factors were as follows:

TABLE XL

RELATIVE IMPORTANCE OF FACTORS IN RANKING
OCCUPATIONS IN AHMEDABAD TEXTILE MILLS

Factor	Relative Weight
Responsibility for equipment	26.3
Skill	23.7
Mental effort	19.9
Responsibility for material	18.8
Responsibility for work of others	10.3
Hazards	0.5
Working conditions	0.5
Physical effort	0.2

[3] Kamla Chowdry and V. R. Trivedi, "Job Evaluation, An Analysis of the Existing Structure in the Ahmedabad Textile Industry," *ATIRA Research Notes*, Vol. III, No. 6 (Oct. 1953).

As Chowdry and Trivedi point out: "In India, where the value of capital goods, like machinery, etc. is rated higher than in a country like the United States, the weights given to the factor of 'responsibility for equipment and process' will be higher than in U.S.A. Again, it is possible that in a country where a very high standard of living and full employment have been achieved, factors like 'physical effort' or 'working conditions' will be weighted higher than in a country like India, because in such countries it would be difficult to find workers who are willing to work in non-congenial environments, unless sufficiently compensated.[4]

"In India, the allocation of machines depends on getting the highest machine efficiency, whereas in U.S.A., the allocation depends on getting the highest man efficiency."[5]

In this study, with a careful procedure in which detailed job descriptions and suggestive guides for ranking was used, it was found necessary to get different judges for each department and to refrain from cross-departmental comparisons. One would expect even more difficulty in a scale designed to cover many industries.

For these reasons, then, we return to wages as a system of ranking, stripping off the dearness allowance and other extras, the seniority increments and the idiosyncratic effects of past market conditions. This leaves the basic wage allotted to an occupation for those first entering the job. And since even the starting basic wages are subject to minor variations as a result of market conditions, the history of the company, and collective bargaining pressures, the occupations have been grouped into broad skill levels or wage slabs, as they are called, based upon the starting basic wage

[4] *Ibid.*, p. 7.
[5] *Ibid.*, p. 11.

allocated to each occupation in the company's standing orders or labor contract. The wage slabs used in four of the factories are given in Table XLI.

TABLE XLI

MINIMUM BASIC MONTHLY WAGE FOR SKILL CLASSES
OF P & M WORKERS, BY FACTORY

Paper		Engine		Biscuit		Rubber	
Class	Wage	Class	Wage	Class	Wage	Class	Wage
A	26/–	Basic	26/–	Unskilled	26/–	Unskilled	26/–
B	32/8	5B	32/5	Semiskilled B	35/–	Semiskilled	35/–
C	39/–	5A	35/8	Semiskilled A	40/–	Skilled B	50/–
D	42/4	4C	37/8	Skilled B	45/–	Skilled A	70/–
E	52/–	4B	42/2	Skilled A	55/–	Highly Skilled	100/–
F	76/–	4A	52/–				
		3B	58/5				
		3A	65/–				
		2A	78/–				
		1	91/–				

In the Type A paper, biscuit, and rubber factories, the company-union agreement on wages specified which jobs fell in which wage class. In the Type C engine factory, with its greater range of skills and highly differentiated classification, the occupational titles were more generic—lathe operator, turner, fitter, wireman, welder, shaper, etc.—and within these designations all or most of the skill classes were to be found. Each worker was given a skill ranking on the basis of the particular job he was doing, even though the title of his occupation would not change.

A glance at the four company rankings shows a clear tendency to separate the class boundaries by multiples of five and ten, and I have adopted a relatively simple cross-company scheme which takes advantage of the common administrative taste for neatness. The classifications in each company were refashioned to make five skill grades, as follows:

Class I	Rs. 62 and over
Class II	Rs. 52—61
Class III	Rs. 42—51
Class IV	Rs. 32—41
Class V	Rs. 31 and under

The P & M occupations within each factory were then placed in one or another category on the basis of the starting wage assigned to that job title at the time of the study. In the case of the engine factory, individuals, not job titles, were assigned to grades. The Type B textile mill did not use the slab system. Each worker in the 120 or so separate occupations in the textile mill is paid according to a designated time wage or piece rate without the over-all structure of wage slabs. For our purposes, however, it was relatively simple to sort the time-rate occupations into the skill grades derived from the other factories. Piece rate jobs were placed into the grades according to the current mean basic wage earned in each job, calculated from the company records.

TABLE XLII

PERCENTAGES OF TOTAL WORKERS IN OCCUPATIONAL CLASSES AND SKILL GRADES

	Textile	Paper	Engine	Biscuit	Rubber
Clerk	3.6	4.8	8.6	11.3	8.5
Supervisor	3.6	6.3	3.6	7.6	2.4
Skilled I	—	6.4	8.5	—	3.5
Skilled II	2.9	2.4	4.3	5.0	2.6
Semiskilled III	43.5	8.0	29.0	4.1	3.5
Semiskilled IV	10.0	28.8	17.9	24.8	6.1
Unskilled V	36.4	43.2	28.1	47.2	73.4
Number	2342	603	614	159	531

GRAPHS 6 through 10: Percent of Workers in Occupational Classes

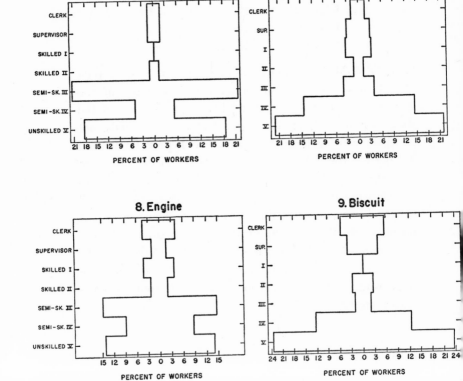

6. Textile

CLERK
SUPERVISOR
SKILLED I
SKILLED II
SEMI-SK. III
SEMI-SK. IV
UNSKILLED V

21 18 15 12 9 6 3 0 3 6 9 12 15 18 21
PERCENT OF WORKERS

7. Paper

CLERK
SUR.
I
II
III
IV
V

21 18 15 12 9 6 3 0 3 6 9 12 15 18 21
PERCENT OF WORKERS

8. Engine

CLERK
SUPERVISOR
SKILLED I
SKILLED II
SEMI-SK. III
SEMI-SK. IV
UNSKILLED V

15 12 9 6 3 0 3 6 9 12 15
PERCENT OF WORKERS

9. Biscuit

CLERK
SUP.
I
II
III
IV
V

24 21 18 15 12 9 6 3 0 3 6 9 12 15 18 21 24
PERCENT OF WORKERS

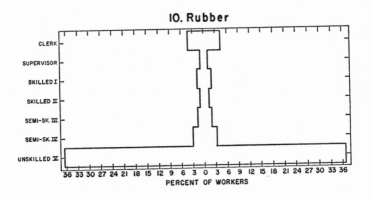

10. Rubber

CLERK
SUPERVISOR
SKILLED I
SKILLED II
SEMI-SK. III
SEMI-SK. IV
UNSKILLED V

36 33 30 27 24 21 18 15 12 9 6 3 0 3 6 9 12 15 18 21 24 27 30 33 36
PERCENT OF WORKERS

Leaving aside for a moment the clerks and supervisor, we see in Table XLII and Graphs 6 to 10 a much more revealing picture of the comparative skill structures in the various factories than was possible in Table XXXIX and Graphs 1 to 5. They bring out the basically flat structure with the thin column of skilled workers rising from an extended base of unskilled workers of the Type A factories as seen in Graphs 7, 9 and 10. In Table XLII we see that most of the workers are in unskilled grade (V). If we combine grade V with the lowest semi-skilled grade (IV), we include about three-fourths of all the workers in each of the three factories—paper, biscuit and rubber. The higher skill levels of the workers in the Type B textile mill and the Type C engine factory as compared with those in any of the Type A factories is quickly apparent. In both the textile mill and the engine factory workers at grade IV or below comprise less than half of the total workforce.

Graphs 6 and 8 bring out more clearly than did the total wage distributions shown in Graphs 1 and 3 the differences in internal structure between Type B and Type C. The textile mill has almost half of its workers in the highest semi-skilled grade (III) and relatively few at the very high skill levels, while the engine factory has a much more even distribution up through the skill hierarchy, with fully 8.5 per cent at the highest skill grade, as compared with none in the textile mill. If we compare the general outlines of Graphs 1 through 5 with those in Graphs 6 through 10, the blurring effect of dearness allowances and seniority increases on skill gradations is clearly apparent, particularly in the way in which the lowest skill categories blend into the semi-skilled levels in the total wage distribution. This is a by-product of the mildness of the progression in D.A.

and seniority increments, and has the effect of making occupational status gradations very imperfectly related to actual wages. Minor movements up the occupational ladder, therefore, have little other than symbolic effect insofar as wages are concerned.

Clerks and Supervisors[6]

Differences among the factories in the number and use of clerks and, even more surprising, of supervisors did not coincide so much with our production system typology as with the dichotomy of new and old factories, and with idiosyncratic features peculiar to each factory.

Except for the biscuit factory, the overhead load of clerks and supervisors was fairly uniform among the companies, averaging about 9.4 per cent of the total workforce. However, in the biscuit company, the clerks and supervisors were almost 10 per cent more numerous, so distorting the occupational structure that there was a clerk or a supervisor for about every four workers. This situation apparently resulted from the twin processes of automation and selective retrenchment discussed in a previous section in connection with the relationship between wages and seniority. In the retrenchment process the supervisory and clerical staff remained almost intact while the laborers were displaced. By way of contrast, the rubber factory also had mostly new, automatic equipment but it did not inherit a workforce structure from an early, more manual operation. The proportion of supervisors (2.4 per cent) was the lowest of the five factories, and the combined

[6] I shall refer to the division of the workforce into clerks, supervisors, and production and maintenance workers as occupational classes to distinguish them from the skill grades, all of which lie within the P & M worker class. When referring to both classes and grades, I shall use the term category.

124

supervisory and clerical overhead was about the same as in the rest of the factories.

While the combined clerical and supervisory overhead was similar among the factories, the proportions of that overhead that were clerical differed radically. In the two older factories, the textile and paper mills, the supervisors were equal or greater in number than the clerks. In the newer factories, clerks were one and one-half to three times as numerous as supervisors. This differential apportionment of the overhead is reflected in the relative wages paid to the two groups.

TABLE XLIII

MEAN CURRENT MONTHLY WAGES BY OCCUPATIONAL CLASS, BY FACTORY

Occupational Class	Textile Rs.	Paper Rs.	Engine Rs.	Biscuit Rs.	Rubber Rs.	All Factories Rs.
Supervisor	147.1	142.2	308.0	185.4	218.5	175.2
Clerk	166.1	153.0	178.9	134.8	119.4	157.7
P & M workers[a]	87.4	82.6	91.3	74.1	65.0	83.3
All workers	92.4	89.7	106.0	89.4	73.4	91.0

[a] Includes temporary workers.

It can be seen that in the older factories where supervisors equalled or outnumbered clerks, their average monthly wages were lower than those of the clerks. In those factories where supervisors were fewer than the clerks, their average monthly wages were considerably higher.

The different general wage levels in the various factories were reflected in the mean wages of each occupational class. But what is most interesting is the difference among the factories in the comparative advantage enjoyed by clerks and supervisors over P & M workers.

TABLE XLIV

MEAN CURRENT MONTHLY WAGES OF CLERKS AND SUPERVISORS
IN RATIO TO THOSE OF P & M WORKERS, BY FACTORY

Factory	Clerks P & M Workers	Supervisors P & M Workers
Textile	1.9	1.7
Paper	1.9	1.7
Engine	2.0	3.4
Biscuit	1.8	2.5
Rubber	1.9	3.4
All factories	1.9	2.1

The all-factories ratios of comparative advantage of the two parts of the overhead, clerks and supervisors versus P & M workers were not too far apart, 1.9 and 2.1 respectively, with supervisors having a slight edge. But an examination of the two columns reveals that the clerks had a highly uniform advantage, earning on the average about twice as much as the average laborer in each factory, while the supervisors ranged from a little more than one and one-half to a little less than three and one-half times as much. Clearly, then, the wage advantage of the clerical group was fairly fixed, while the companies' valuation of the supervisory personnel varied considerably: the two older companies (Types A and B) give them little comparative advantage, less than the clerks, while the three newer factories (Types A and C) gave them much more.

The reason for this differential assessment is that the older factories sprinkled supervisors well down through the production process, frequently having them engage in processing and producing goods themselves. In these factories the highest skilled laborers earned more than many of the workers designated as supervisors. In the textile mill, for instance, a fitter in the ring-fix department earned a basic wage of Rs. 78, while a jobber in the calendering section got only Rs. 52 or in the bleaching department only Rs. 45/8. The same situation held true in the paper mill where a mason, blacksmith, ruler and binder, electrician, or fitter made as much as a foreman and more than an assistant foreman. The supervisors in the two older factories were paid more than the workers in their particular division, but in the plant-wide hierarchy many of them rank below the highly skilled non-supervisory personnel. The same situation held, but to a considerably lesser extent, in the biscuit factory and explains the ratio of mean wage for supervisors two and one-half times as high as the P & M workers' mean wage, a ratio which falls between the low ratio of the older factories and high ratio in the newer ones. It will be recalled that the biscuit factory is also intermediate in the number of years it has been in operation. In the engine and rubber factories the division between supervisor and P & M worker is a clear one. In both factories all supervisors are paid higher wages than all P & M workers, a fact reflected in the much higher wage ratio.

To recapitulate: the supervisory and clerical overhead seems to be relatively constant at about ten per cent. Clerks were paid on the average twice as much as the P & M workers in all five factories, but the supervisors varied in two patterns, one a superior cadre well above both clerks and P & M workers and the other a group some of whose members intermingled with the laborers. In the latter case, the mean wage for the clerks was higher than that of the supervisors and they represented a smaller proportion of the total workforce; in the former case, the reverse is true. Here is a difference that might well have been expected to follow the production system typology, but which did not; rather, it coincided simply with the different ages of the factories.

The uniformity in clerical wages lies not only in their relationship to P & M wage levels but also in absolute terms. The difference among companies in mean wages of clerks was not statistically significant ($F = 2.17$, $df = 4$, $p > .05$). This is not surprising inasmuch as the job lies outside of the manufacturing process and does not change radically with the product being manufactured or with the general social structure of the factory. Not only is the clerical class fairly uniform from factory to factory, but within the factory it is an isolated unit which replaces itself from outside rather than from within the factory ranks. Only 11 of the sample of 80 clerks had held any non-clerical job at all within the factory, and of these 11 only two had worked in the production process (one was a P & M worker who reached the lowest level of the clerical hierarchy called semi-clerical, and the other was a line supervisor who had moved into the highly paid auditor's job rather than into straight clerical work). The remaining nine had worked in various service jobs such as office boy, dispatcher, general apprentice, timekeeper, etc. In short, once someone was employed in the shop, his chances of crossing the line into the clerical ranks were very slim indeed. Nor do those hired as clerks move out into other sections of the factory. Only 4 supervisors out of 169 in all factories had been clerks and no P & M worker had been a clerk.

Within the clerical enclave itself, there were various gradations. At the bottom was the semi-clerical worker whose desk, if any, was on the shop floor and who recorded the result of the production process as it occurred. This rank was found only in the older factories, the textile and paper mills. Next came the bulk of the clerks normally divided into two layers, Junior and Senior Grade, plus a Chief Clerk. Above these were a greater or lesser number of specialized clerical jobs such as accountant, auditor, secretary, and cashier, who were paid wages higher than the senior grade clerks.

Upward mobility theoretically takes place from the junior to the senior layers, then either into chief clerk or one of the specialized posts. At the upper reaches, the clerical ladder could theoretically lead into the company officer rank, but in family-run firms this is unlikely. Upward mobility among clerks, however, was more theoretical than real, as an examination of the work careers of the clerks revealed. Job openings, no matter at what level, are usually filled from outside the factory rather than from the ranks of the clerks within. In at least one factory, the biscuit factory, the dichotomy of junior and senior clerk was based on whether the individual passed his matriculation examination at the end of his high school training, a division hardly conducive to upward mobility based upon work accomplishment.

The general picture, then, is static. Turnover is low. The clerks have more seniority than the factory average in every company. Upward mobility is slight. Only six out of the eighty clerks in the sample had current clerical designations different from the ones they had when they entered the firm. Insulation from the rest of the workforce is relatively complete. In the factory, clerks represent the petty literati class with all of the status and role consequences that that term implies. As we shall see, the primary differentiation of the clerks is on the basis of social characteristics, and paramount among these is literacy in English.

Internal Mobility

So far in this chapter we have been looking at each of the five factories in cross-section, examining and contrasting certain aspects of the organization of its labor force, particularly its over-all wage and skill structure and the nature of the overhead load of clerks and supervisors. We are now in the position to add to our picture a longitudinal dimension, the work careers of the individual employees and, more specifically, we may ask two related questions: to what extent are the organizational structures static or composed of many moving parts; and to what extent is any movement horizontal or vertical? Let us attack these questions in reverse order.

To assay the extent of vertical mobility we use the basic starting wage slab, which allows us to make comparative statements about the degree of mobility in each factory. Tables XLV through XLIX are matrices that indicate the workers' entry job class or skill grades cross-tabulated with their current job class or grades. For instance, reading a few entries in Table XLV from the figure in the upper left corner we see that 85 out of the 86 who started as clerks in the textile mill are still clerks and that all 85 held this position when they were first hired; or, from the figure in the lower right corner, we see that 825 out of 976 workers who entered the textile mill as unskilled P & M workers are still in that class. The figures in the diagonals represent stability, that is those workers who are now at the same job class or grade as they were when they entered the factory. Except for the clerk and supervisor categories, whose relative ranking varies among the factories as we point out above, any frequencies above the diagonal represent downward mobility and those below the diagonal upward mobility.

Table L gives summary figures on occupational mobility in the five factories. Looking at row three, we see most workers in all factories are currently employed at their entry jobs, that most of those who come into the factory as unskilled workers stay here, and that in most factories when occupational changes do occur they tend to cross class lines. The over-all impression one gains from looking at Tables XLV through XLIX is one of stability, expressed in the heavy predominance of the diagonals. The corollary of this stability is that the factories tend to recruit externally for skilled employees instead of moving personnel internally. The portions on either side of the diagonals indicate that vertical class mobility, when it does occur, is almost entirely upward.

Aside from these generalizations that apply to all of the factories, the most interesting findings emerge from a comparison of the five factories. To assist in this comparison,

TABLE XLV

CURRENT AND ENTRY JOB CATEGORIES OF ALL WORKERS IN TEXTILE MILL

Entry Job Category	Current Job Category							
	Clerk	Sup.	I	II	III	IV	V	Total
Clerk	85	1						86
Sup.		36						36
I			–					–
II				41				41
III		24			935			959
IV		10		14	14	179	27	244
V		13		14	69	55	825	976
Total	85	84	–	69	1018	234	852	2342

TABLE XLVI

CURRENT AND ENTRY JOB CATEGORIES OF ALL WORKERS IN PAPER MILL

Entry Job Category	Current Job Category							
	Clerk	Sup.	I	II	III	IV	V	Total
Clerk	23	1						24
Sup.		6						6
I			34					34
II		1		15				16
III					19			19
IV		6			10	135		151
V	6	24	5		19	39	260	353
Total	29	38	39	15	48	174	260	603

TABLE XLVII

CURRENT AND ENTRY JOB CATEGORIES FOR ALL WORKERS IN THE ENGINE FACTORY

Entry Job Category	Current Job Category							
	Clerk	Sup.	I	II	III	IV	V	Total
Clerk	45	2						47
Sup.		6						6
I		4	16					20
II		6	16	16				38
III		3	16	5	52			76
IV				5	10	58		73
V	8	1	5		115	52	173	354
Total	53	22	53	26	177	110	173	614

we have converted the absolute figures in the diagonals of the matrices into percentages; that is, Table LI gives the percentage of each current job category occupied by immobiles.

It will be noted immediately that there is considerable range in the proportion of workers at all levels who are

132

TABLE XLVIII

CURRENT AND ENTRY JOB CATEGORIES FOR ALL WORKERS IN THE BISCUIT FACTORY

Entry Job Category	Current Job Category							
	Clerk	Sup.	I	II	III	IV	V	Total
Clerk	17							17
Sup.		7						7
I			–					–
II				7			1	8
III					5			5
IV	1	2				24	1	28
V		3			1	17	73	94
Total	18	12	–	7	6	41	75	159

TABLE XLIX

CURRENT AND ENTRY JOB CATEGORIES FOR ALL WORKERS IN THE RUBBER FACTORY

Entry Job Class or Grade	Current Job Class/Grade							
	Clerk	Sup.	I	II	III	IV	V	Total
Clerk	35							35
Sup.	2	8						10
I		1	14					15
II				14				14
III					14			14
IV						23		23
V	8	4	5		5	9	389	420
Total	45	13	19	14	19	32	389	531

TABLE L

SUMMARY OF PERCENTAGE OF MOBILES AMONG ALL WORKERS, BY FACTORY

Mobile	Textile	Paper	Engine	Biscuit	Rubber
Inter-category	10.3	17.5	39.8	17.0	6.3
Intra-category	7.0	5.6	4.1	7.5	11.7
Any job change	17.3	23.1	43.9	24.5	18.0

TABLE LI

PERCENTAGE OF WORKERS CURRENTLY IN EACH OCCUPATIONAL
CATEGORY HIRED INTO THAT CATEGORY

Current Job Category	Textile	Paper	Engine	Biscuit	Rubber
Clerk	100.0	80.0	84.8	94.4	78.3
Supervisor	42.9	15.8	27.3	58.3	61.5
I	—	87.5	30.0	—	100.0
II	59.4	100.0	60.0	100.0	100.0
III	91.9	40.0	29.4	80.0	75.0
IV	76.5	80.6	57.1	56.7	71.4
V	96.8	100.0	100.0	96.5	100.0
All levels	89.7	82.5	60.2	83.0	93.7

immobiles—from 60.2 per cent in the relatively mobile engine factory to 93.7 per cent in the almost completely static rubber factory. The other three factories lie in between, but closer to the static than the mobile end of the continuum. This difference in internal vertical mobility rates derives in part from the following factors: the skill hierarchy, workforce stability, and external recruitment.

Skill Hierarchy

The difference in the percentage of immobiles between the Type C engine factory and the Type A rubber factory can partially be explained by a glance at Graphs 8 through 10, which depict the distribution of their skill grades. The exaggerated slab structure of the rubber factory with almost three-fourths of its workers in the unskilled grade presents very little opportunity indeed for workers to move upward in the skill hierarchy, while the more evenly distributed skill hierarchy of the engine factory, and in particular its high percentage of Grade III semi-skilled workers, presents many more opportunities. Graphs 7 and 9 show that the other two Type A factories, the paper and biscuit companies, fall between the engine and rubber factories in their departure from the slab structure as well as in their percentages of immobiles. On the basis of the dispersion of the skill hierarchy, the surprising finding is the high rate of immobility in the Type B textile mill. Its workers are almost as immobile as those in the rubber factory, while its skill hierarchy, seen in Graph 6, is much more dispersed. To explain this anomaly we shall have to examine the other two factors, workforce stability and external recruitment, and we shall take a closer look at the differential immobility rates by skill grade.

In one sense, the dispersion of the skill structure might be thought of as a basic element in the provision of opportunity for advancement. Another element, of course, is the rate at which posts become vacant. In turn, this depends in part on fluctuations in the total size of the workforce in a given factory and in part upon the turnover rates. Based upon our sequence of immobility rates, we would expect the rubber factory to have the highest seniority and the most even total labor force, while the engine factory should have low seniority and rapid expansion. The other factories should fall in between. Neither of these conditions obtains. The median seniority by companies is highest for the paper mill with 14.6 years, and lowest with the rubber factory with 1.8 years; the textile, biscuit and engine factories lie in the middle with 9.4, 8.1 and 5.0 years, respectively.

It will be recalled that we showed earlier that seniority of the workers was inextricably bound with and compounded by the company's history of over-all stability in the size of its workforce. If we return to Table XXX, which gives the total number of workers in each factory in the years since 1950, we can see whether such differences can

135

account for the variations in the internal mobility among the factories. A comparison of the columns in Table XXX does not suggest a clear relationship between workforce stability and vertical immobility rates. The immobile rubber factory and the mobile engine factory have both had a fairly even rate of expansion, and each has had one year of contraction of its total labor force. But perhaps the contrast is too great between the Type A rubber factory and the Type C engine factory to permit the effect of workforce stability to be apparent. The same lack of direct relationship occurs in the comparison between the paper and biscuit factories, both Type A: they have about the same immobility rates, while the paper mill has had a very slight growth in total labor force and the biscuit factory has had a sharp decline in total number of workers. More interesting is the comparison between the Type C engine factory and the Type B textile mill. The textile mill had a very recent (1955-56) sudden expansion in the total number of workers when it opened another shift operation, and this expansion in both relative and absolute terms exceeded the expansion of the engine factory. And yet the immobility rate of the textile mill was 89.7 per cent as compared with 60.2 per cent in the engine factory.

If these two structural features, skill hierarchy and workforce stability, are not sufficient to explain differences in the over-all immobility rates, the answer must lie in the extent to which skilled jobs in each factory tend to be filled by external recruitment or internal promotion. This will be the result both of a company preference and the general availability of relevant skills in the labor market at large. At this point it is well to realize that the immobiles represented in the diagonals of the matrices given in Tables XLV through XLIX and in the percentages in Table

L also represent the number of workers who were externally recruited in each job category. It can be seen that all of the factories except the engine factory tend to recruit their skilled and semi-skilled workers from outside. Those coming in as unskilled workers tend to remain at this level. Only about 50 per cent of those who entered as unskilled workers have remained there in the engine factory, while in the rubber factory it was 93 per cent, in the textile mill 85 per cent, in the biscuit factory 77 per cent, and in the paper mill 75 per cent. In the three Type A factories, the skilled workers are of a different character than the unskilled laborers and represent a distinct minority of the workforce. The primary production process is carried on largely by workers classified as unskilled. It is therefore not surprising that skilled labor is set apart from unskilled labor. In fact, in two of the three Type A factories some of the highest skilled workers are ethnically separate and drawn from other regions of the country—Uttar Pradesh for the paper mill and Bengal for the rubber factory.

The more crucial contrast, however, lies between the Type B textile mill and the Type C engine factory. The contrast between these two factories is very clear. To rule out the effect of the difference in turnover rates and the greater longevity of the textile mill as compared with the engine factory, let us examine the occupational categories of the new employees hired during the five years preceding the study, 1952-56 inclusive. In the engine factory 75 per cent of these new employees entered into Classes IV and V, the unskilled and lowest semi-skilled grades; whereas 52.8 per cent of the new workers in the textile mill entered Grade III, the higher semi-skilled grade. In both companies, the largest proportions of the workers were in Grade III, and in the textile mill 92.9 per cent of these workers were externally recruited, while only 29.4 per cent of them were so recruited in the engine factory.

Having made these general contrasts in the factors contributing to the differences in the over-all vertical mobility rates among companies, we can now turn to a sketch of the over-all patterns of recruitment and vertical mobility at all skill levels. As we noted before, the clerks form a separate labor pool with little exchange of personnel with other elements in the factory. The supervisors, as we also have noted, sometimes reach down and overlap the topmost skill categories, both in wages and in prestige, but as a class they have been treated in tabular presentations as at the top of the skill hierarchy. The skill gradations among P & M workers, based upon wage slabs, ranged in order from the highest skilled to the least skilled down through the non-permanent workers. While this might seem like a continuous hierarchy, in fact there are discontinuities, gaps, and barriers which make it very unlikely that any individual will follow a course from the lowest skilled grade, through the succeeding skill grades, up to the supervisory level. These gaps and barriers vary by factory type, but tend to produce several relatively separate labor pools and channels of upward mobility in each factory.

In the three Type A factories—paper, biscuit and rubber —skill Grades I and II are externally recruited. They make up less than 10 per cent of the workforce and bring in technical and artisan skills which are not likely to be gained by experience in the factory. None of the supervisors in these factories entered or passed through skill Grade I or II, and almost none of those currently in these levels served in any other grade. Internally-recruited supervisors jump over this artisan hurdle. The key to upward mobility lies in the nature of skill Grade III. In the biscuit and rubber factories, most workers in this grade were recruited externally, as were most of the supervisors. In the paper mill, where this grade is recruited internally, the path is clear into the supervisory levels, and most of the supervisors come from the company's own ranks.

In the Type B textile mill there were a few workers in skill Grade I, but none of them appeared in the sample, and skill Grade II served the same function and had the same origins as it did in the Type A factories. Those who became supervisors jumped over this grade and came in equal numbers from Grade III and Grades IV and V combined. The textile mill in general, with its 120 or so highly specialized occupational titles and low internal mobility (intra-category job changes add only 7 per cent to the total job changes), resembles nothing so much as a vertical bank of pigeonholes in which there is a constant movement in and out of the company in a horizontal direction, but very little movement vertically. Its outline approximates the diamond shaped model, while the Type C engine factory resembles most clearly the true pyramidal structure. The bulk of the supervisors are drawn from the skilled and semi-skilled grades within the factory and not recruited directly as supervisors. Each category draws a relatively high proportion of its occupants from the category below it. It is clear that the engine factory, with its high mobility and internal upgrading of skills, is, unlike the textile mill, carrying the burden of educating its own labor force and in particular its own highly skilled workers.

Having outlined the general social organization of the workforce in the five factories, particularly their hierarchical orderings, we shall turn in the next chapter to the way in which different workers fit into that structure and their reactions to it.

SUMMARY

The textile mill and the engine factory were found to have departed more from the traditional social organization than the Type A factories in that they are less primary-group organized, more complex in their division of labor, and have more interdependence of roles. The wage hierarchies were found to reflect differences among the three types of factories. However, the occupational and skill structures are obscured by dearness allowances, seniority increments, and idiosyncratic market considerations, so a skill classification based upon a system of blocks of starting wages was developed. This system showed clearly the slab outline of the Type A factories, the more diamond-shaped Type B factory, and the pyramidal Type C factory.

The supervisory and clerical overhead is relatively constant at about ten per cent of the workforce in each factory. The clerks are a separate group, similar in income in all factories, with little interchange with other occupational classes and little internal mobility. Supervisors in the newer factories are a superior elite above both clerks and production and maintenance workers; in the older factories they extend well down into the production process itself.

Vertical mobility, uncommon in all factories, is found most frequently in the Type C factory. The three factory types differ in their paths of possible upward mobility.

CHAPTER V · THE WORKER AND
THE HIERARCHY

❚❘❚❘❚ NOW THAT we have described the hierarchical organization of the factories, we can turn our attention again to the individual workers who fit into that organization. In this chapter, we shall ask a number of related questions: How do the workers in the various occupational categories differ from one another? Are the main distinguishing attributes those which reflect status gradations in the external society? Do they have to do with the worker's job history in his present factory? To what extent do workers aspire to higher rank in the hierarchy and what distinguishes those who aspire from those who do not? Do status differentials reflect themselves in a greater or lesser degree of favorableness toward the company? To what extent do the factories differ from one another in the answers to all of these questions? Do such differences coincide with our production system or our old versus new typologies? And, finally, at a more general level, we shall consider whether the nature of status in the factories seems to reflect another element in the social transformation described in the Introduction: a shift from ascribed to achieved status.

SOCIAL CHARACTERISTICS AND OCCUPATIONAL CLASS

Let us start our examination of the parallels between the attributes of status in the general society and in the factories with the broadest status differentials within the factories—the occupational classes—and with those social characteristics that are most qualitative—that is, status attributes that describe a person but do not fix him as high

141

or low in the prestige hierarchy. We shall then proceed to the variables that rank an individual in the general society and at the same time refine our status gradient within the factory to include the P & M skill grades as well as the occupational classes, or in some cases current wage differences.

Family

Variations in the first set of social characteristics—attributes of the family—if they have any relevance at all, might conceivably be thought of more as a by-product of the factory than as potential determinants of intra-factory status. Table LII enumerates various attributes of the families of the workers in each occupational class in the combined workforce.[1]

TABLE LII

SELECTED FAMILY CHARACTERISTICS BY OCCUPATIONAL
CLASS IN ALL FACTORIES

Characteristic	Clerks	Supervisors	P & M Workers
Per cent single	20.9	11.8	26.3
Mean number in household	5.9	5.5	5.1
Per cent spouses employed	9.7	2.7	7.0
Mean number of dependents per earner	3.0	3.1	2.6
Mean per capita income (Rs.)	41.1	46.7	29.1

The differences in the family styles can be seen from Table LII. Although one-fifth of the clerks have never married, they tend to come from larger households than

---

[1] Detailed tables for each family characteristic, by factory, are given in Appendix C.

the other classes of workers. Their extra income from the relatively high proportion of working spouses (9.7 per cent) is partially absorbed by a high dependency load. While this does not bring the per capita income of the clerks down to that of the P & M workers, it does reduce their current wage, which is almost twice as high as the P & M workers' (see Table XLIII), to a point where it is only about 40 per cent higher. The supervisors' current wage advantage is also drastically reduced; the mean current wage of supervisors is 210 per cent of the P & M mean current wage, while the mean per capita income of supervisors is only 160 per cent. Again, the greater size of household and greater dependency load of the supervisors compared with those of P & M workers explains the reduction. In contrast to the clerks, however, the supervisors have a high proportion of non-working spouses; their high dependency load does not force wives to work. The most striking thing about the P & M worker is that more than one-fourth have never married.

In general, then, the association of occupational class with family characteristics reflects the tendency we noted earlier for above average incomes to attract dependent kin. While we noted in Chapter II that the increased dependency load tended to reduce the average factory worker's family's per capita income to that of the general Poona population, and it also tended to reduce differences in current wages among the factories, its influence is not enough to completely obliterate (although it shrinks) per capita income differences among the occupational classes.

Sex

Out of the thirty females in the sample, there were no clerks or supervisors. All were in the unskilled ranks of the P & M workers.

143

Extra-Local Origins

It is conceivable that the factories might either penalize or reward more highly skilled workers from outside the city, from outside the region, or whose mother tongue was other than Marathi. Table LIII indicates the proportion of workers who have each degree of "foreignness" in each occupational class.[2]

TABLE LIII

PERCENTAGES OF "ALIEN" WORKERS BY DEGREE
AND OCCUPATIONAL CLASS

	Clerks	Supervisors	P & M Workers
Non-Poona	73.7	66.2	69.5
Non-Maharashtrian	31.9	58.6	40.0
Non-Marathi speaking	20.8	15.2	22.8

There does not appear to be a very significant association between Poona or Maharashtra origin and occupational class. The surprisingly high figure of about 60 per cent of the supervisors coming from outside Maharashtra is the result of the numerical predominance in the total sample of supervisors in the textile mill, which, as we have seen, draws experienced workers from a wide area. That this is an exaggeration of the degree of "alienness" of the supervisors may be seen from the fact that only 15 per cent spoke as their mother tongue a language other than Marathi.

To test further the relevance of "alienness", measures of association between skill grade and each of the above variables were computed. Although, as we have noted

[2] The detailed tables on each degree of "foreignness" by occupational class and by factory are given in Appendix D.

earlier, several of the factories recruited specific types of skilled workers from places as far away as Bengal and Uttar Pradesh, no over-all association between any degree of alienness and rank was found among the P & M workers.

Age

Age, like sex, is a social characteristic that in traditional Indian society acts as a prime determinant of an individual's personal status within the framework of his more general status, based on the groups with which he is affiliated. Unlike their counterparts in some Western countries, where obsolescence and the decline of respect start early, most Indian adult males in the traditional kin-organized work situation find through most of life that their status increases with age, and few authority lines reverse the age gradient. This, of course, is not likely to be nearly so perfectly realized in a factory with so many other status determinants at work, but it is interesting to see to what extent age and position coincide in the factory hierarchy. Since, as we noted in Chapter II, age distributions differ considerably from factory to factory and, as we noted in Chapter IV, the distributions of workers in various occupational categories also differ, the age comparisons must be made within each factory separately. Table LIV gives the mean ages of the three broad occupational classes.

TABLE LIV

MEAN AGES OF OCCUPATIONAL CLASSES BY FACTORY

Occupational Class	Textile	Paper	Engine	Biscuit	Rubber	All Factories
Clerks	43.1	44.0	33.4	40.9	34.4	39.1
Supervisors	34.9	29.8	29.1	27.9	29.8	31.1
P & M workers	35.4	34.6	28.1	30.9	25.5	32.8

It will be noted that the clerks in each factory are uniformly older on the average than either the supervisors or the P & M workers, which reflects greater seniority and lower turnover in this class. The comparison between the supervisors and P & M workers is not so clear-cut. In the engine and rubber factories the supervisors are slightly older, and in the other factories they are younger than the P & M workers. But in all, the difference is small enough for us to be certain that the authority gradient very often contravenes the age hierarchy. If we leave authority aside and confine ourselves to the P & M class, we can examine the correlation between status within the factory and age more directly. Table LV gives the Pearsonian correlation coefficients for the relationship between age and current wages for permanent workers. Temporary and *badli* workers were omitted because their wages were too variable to permit a meaningful comparison.

TABLE LV

CORRELATION BETWEEN AGE AND CURRENT WAGE OF
PERMANENT P & M WORKERS, BY FACTORY

Factory	Correlation
Textile	—.11
Paper	+.19
Engine	+.78*
Biscuit	+.42*
Rubber	+.33*

* Significant at the $p < .01$ level.

An examination of the table indicates that age is correlated significantly with wages only in the engine, biscuit and rubber factories. This difference among factories does not correspond with our production process typology, although we might expect that age and wages would correlate most highly in the Type A factories, while in the Type B and C other status determinants, including skill and experience, would take precedence over age. What seems to be the case, however, is that the correlation is substantial only in the newer factories that have been in operation only for a few years and where the average age is relatively low. This suggests the possibility that as these newer factories mature and their workers get older, they, too, will find that age and standing in the factory will no longer be associated.

While we have been dealing with age as an independent social characteristic, it is, of course, inextricably bound up with seniority in both the labor force at large and in the factories under study. The three variables are, however, by no means completely corresponding, and we shall discuss seniority separately when we turn to the status-enhancing properties of work experience.

Caste, Literacy in English, Education

If one were to select three primary criteria of urban stratification in India, they would be ethnic group, literacy, and education. Most other variables measuring social status would correlate with one or more of these. While, as will be demonstrated, the three are highly intercorrelated, they represent an important contrast in the forms of status-giving attributes both in terms of sociological theory and of the character of Indian society in general. Ethnic group affiliation, including caste, is fixed at birth and is the proto-type of ascribed status characteristics. Education and liter-acy in English, on the other hand, are the chief examples in most western societies of achieved status attributes. As we noted in the introduction, one of the anticipated

147

consequences of industrialization is a shift from ascribed to achieved status as the primary ranking device within the society at large. From this fundamental change such by-products as individualism, the decline of the joint family, lowering of birth rate, success striving, and many other characteristics attributed to Western society are supposed to flow. We shall discuss at a later point the extent to which status within the factory is based upon achieved attributes in the work experience itself. For the present, however, the discussion will concern the ascribed and achieved status aspects that the worker brings to the factory—ethnic group, literacy in English, and education, and the extent to which they are reflected in different positions within the factories.

As we noted in Table II, some 70 per cent of the workers were literate in Marathi, so this does not serve as a good discriminator of status levels in the factory. Differences of degree in literacy coincide so closely with differences in educational level that they need not be treated separately here. However, literacy in English is an important status determinant in the general society that sets apart a relatively small class with a history of some direct contact with the westernized segment of the culture. Within the factory, it is clearly an important factor in determining the individual's occupational class, as Table LVI indicates.

All but two of the clerks in the sample were literate in English, and these two, one in the paper and one in the biscuit factory, fell at the bottom of the clerical hierarchy, in the semi-clerical class. In all factories more supervisors were literate in English than laborers. Even though Maharashtra is one of the areas in India where constant use of the vernacular among the educated elite is common,

TABLE LVI

PER CENT OF EACH OCCUPATIONAL CLASS
LITERATE IN ENGLISH, BY FACTORY

	Textile	Paper	Engine	Biscuit	Rubber	All Factories
Clerks	100.0	80.0	100.0	94.4	100.0	97.0
Supervisors	26.2	26.3	95.4	75.0	100.0	44.4
Laborers	5.1	13.5	58.3	35.7	40.2	19.2

the factories clearly place a high premium on knowledge of English.

When we consider differences among the factories, the differential advantage of clerks over supervisors and supervisors over P & M workers holds true in all factories. It is clear that the relatively higher educational and literacy level in the newer (engine, biscuit and rubber) factories versus the older (textile and paper) factories is reflected in the greater predominance of workers literate in English in the newer factories in every occupational class.

While literacy in English does serve to sort workers into occupational classes, it does not seem to distribute them into different skill grades. In none of the factories was there a significant association between literacy in English and the skill grades of the P & M workers. To see whether this anomaly—literacy in English distributing workers into occupational classes, but once they fall into the P & M worker category, it is no longer relevant—holds up, let us turn to the more sensitive index, measuring roughly the same variable, education.

A glance at the percentages for the combined factories will show that the educational level of the clerks is higher than that of the supervisors and the educational level of

149

TABLE LVII

EDUCATIONAL LEVEL OF EACH OCCUPATIONAL CLASS, BY FACTORY

Occupational Class	No Education	Non-Matriculate	Matriculate	College	Number in Sample
Textile					
Clerks	—	33.3	44.4	22.2	9
Supervisors	36.9	50.0	6.0	7.1	84
P & M workers	40.5	58.2	0.6	0.6	158
Paper					
Clerks	—	60.0	20.0	20.0	5
Supervisors	23.7	65.8	—	10.5	38
P & M workers	47.7	50.5	—	1.8	111
Engine					
Clerks	—	20.0	64.0	16.0	25
Supervisors	—	50.0	13.6	36.4	22
P & M workers	12.6	66.0	18.4	2.9	103
Biscuit					
Clerks	—	61.1	16.7	22.2	18
Supervisors	—	50.0	25.0	25.0	12
P & M workers	18.4	80.6	1.0	—	98
Rubber					
Clerks	—	21.7	47.8	30.4	23
Supervisors	—	—	61.5	38.5	13
P & M workers	18.6	75.5	5.9	—	102
All Factories[a]					
Clerks	—	33.5	44.3	22.2	80
Supervisors	23.7	49.7	11.2	15.4	169
P & M workers	34.2	61.1	3.7	1.0	572

[a] Weighted by inverse of sampling ratios.

the supervisors higher than that of the P & M workers. The bulk of the clerks have passed their matriculation examination, while most supervisors and P & M workers have not. The educational superiority of the clerks over the supervisors holds in all five factories as does the superiority of the supervisors over the P & M workers. As in the case of literacy in English, the comparative educational level of the clerks and supervisors reflects the same division we found in comparing their total workforces: in the three newer factories—the engine, biscuit, and rubber factories—it is higher than in the older textile and paper mills. In other words, the different factories attract differing educational levels in their workers, sort them out into clerical, supervisory, and P & M levels according to their educational attainments. It will be noted that only in the engine factory, where skill levels are highest, have many (20.3 per cent) of the P & M workers passed their matriculation examination, but in all factories a few have. It will also be noted that only in the older factories are there supervisors with no education whatever, and in the newest factory, the rubber factory, all supervisors are matriculates.

Having reached our expected conclusion that education, like literacy in English, does in fact differentiate among the occupational classes in all factories, let us examine the second part of our proposition: once occupational class assignment has taken place, education does not determine hierarchical position within the class. So that we may examine this hypothesis simultaneously in each class in each factory, Table LVIII presents the mean monthly wage within each educational level by class and by factory.

It will be seen from Table LVIII that the only occupational class where education is clearly associated with higher income is the supervisory. Except for one break in the pattern in the paper factory, the mean wage of supervisors with only primary or no education is lower than that of supervisors with middle and secondary education, and they in turn have a lower mean wage than the matriculates or the college trained. Neither within the clerical nor the P & M group do wage differences march in step with educational differences.

From these data we can conclude that educational

151

TABLE LVIII

MEAN MONTHLY WAGE OF EACH EDUCATIONAL LEVEL
BY OCCUPATIONAL CLASS AND BY FACTORY

	Primary or Less		Secondary		Matriculate or Higher	
	Sample Number	Mean Wage in Rs.	Sample Number	Mean Wage in Rs.	Sample Number	Mean Wage in Rs.
Textile						
Clerks	—	—		168.0	6	166.1
Supervisors	51	128.4	22	141.1	11	245.6
P & M workers	126	87.8	29	82.2	2	142.5
Paper						
Clerks	1	87.0	2	145.0	2	194.0
Supervisors	22	159.1	12	118.9	4	231.2
P & M workers	83	82.9	25	87.9	2	65.0
Engine						
Clerks	—	—	5	233.4	20	165.2
Supervisors	—	—	11	246.8	11	369.1
P & M workers	33	89.2	48	85.2	22	91.3
Biscuit						
Clerks	—	—	11	100.2	7	189.3
Supervisors	—	—	6	108.7	6	262.2
P & M workers	43	74.0	53	78.2	1	125.0
Rubber						
Clerks	—	—	5	85.8	18	128.7
Supervisors	—	—	—	—	13	218.5
P & M workers	49	65.0	45	70.9	5	56.0

attainment is a primary basis of assortment into the broad occupational classes in the factory, but once such an assignment has occurred, educational differences, except for the supervisors, do not produce differences within the broad classes. The exception of the supervisors is a result of the fact that the supervisory class includes a much greater range of skills than the other classes, going from those such as engineers and chemists at the top, for whom formal training is a requirement, to simple gang bosses, for whom it is not. There are in fact few posts within the factory where anything above minimal literacy is used on the job.

Caste and Ethnic Group

Let us turn from these two achieved status attributes to the classic ascribed status attribute, caste or ethnic group. Table LIX shows the distribution of the various groups within each occupational class by factory.

TABLE LIX

PER CENT OF EACH OCCUPATIONAL CLASS IN EACH CASTE OR ETHNIC GROUP, BY FACTORY

	Brahman	Maratha	Intermediate	Village Artisan	Village Servant	Backward Classes	Other Region	Other Religion	Number in Sample
Textile									
Clerks	33.3	44.4	—	—	—	—	22.2	—	9
Supervisors	17.9	47.6	9.5	8.3	7.1	3.6	3.6	2.4	84
P & M workers	2.5	44.9	8.2	7.6	7.6	9.5	9.5	10.1	158
Paper									
Clerks	60.0	—	20.0	20.0	—	—	—	—	5
Supervisors	10.5	31.6	10.5	—	7.9	26.3	5.3	7.9	38
P & M workers	8.1	30.6	9.9	1.8	11.7	23.4	6.3	8.1	111
Engine									
Clerks	92.0	8.0	—	—	—	—	—	—	25
Supervisors	40.9	31.8	4.5	4.5	—	4.5	4.5	9.1	22
P & M workers	31.1	22.3	5.8	6.8	1.0	13.6	5.8	13.6	103
Biscuit									
Clerks	83.3	5.6	—	11.2	—	—	—	—	18
Supervisors	83.3	8.3	—	—	—	—	8.3	—	12
P & M workers	50.0	27.5	7.1	3.1	2.0	3.1	6.1	1.0	98
Rubber									
Clerks	86.4	4.5	4.5	—	4.5	—	—	—	22[a]
Supervisors	58.3	—	—	—	—	—	33.3	8.3	12[a]
P & M workers	24.5	21.6	13.7	2.0	6.9	11.8	8.8	10.8	102
All Factories[b]									
Clerks	64.1	17.8	5.2	3.4	0.8	—	8.2	—	79[a]
Supervisors	26.8	35.7	7.7	4.8	5.4	8.3	6.5	4.8	168[a]
P & M workers	11.6	36.7	8.8	5.8	6.6	12.1	8.3	10.1	572

[a] One worker did not answer question on caste.
[b] Weighted by inverse of sampling ratio.

Table LIX illustrates in a striking fashion the differential reflection of caste within the different occupational levels of the factory. The numerical superiority of Brahmans among the clerks in the combined factory workforce (64.1 per cent) is matched in each of the factories except the textile mill, where Marathas have a slight edge. The caste distribution among the supervisors is more varied. In the older factories—the textile and paper mills—it resembles fairly closely the caste spread among the P & M workers, although in the textile mill there is a higher proportion of Brahmans and a lower proportion of backward castes and non-Maharashtrians among supervisors than among the P & M workers. In all but the paper mill, with its high proportion of P & M workers from tribal groups, the backward class supervisor is a rarity. The importation of skills from Bengal and North India in the rubber factory shows up in the fact that 4 out of 12 supervisors in that factory come from other regions of India.

So far as the hierarchical aspects of caste are concerned, that is, leaving aside people from other regions and other religions, the two most interesting groups are those at the two ends of the hierarchy, the Brahmans and the Backward Classes. Table LIX presents the per cent which each ethnic group comprises of each occupational level. So far as caste is concerned, another type of comparison reveals more clearly the varying concentrations of the two caste groups among the occupational classes. Table LX gives the per cent of each caste group which falls in the different occupational classes.

It is clear that in all factories the bulk of both caste groups are P & M workers, but that in each factory from one-fourth to almost one-half of the Brahmans are either clerks or supervisors. On the other hand, there are no

TABLE LX

PERCENTAGE DISTRIBUTION OF BRAHMANS, BACKWARD CLASSES, AND ALL-CASTES AMONG OCCUPATIONAL CLASSES, BY FACTORY

	Clerks	Supervisors	P & M Workers	Number in Sample
Textile				
Br	28.8	15.3	55.9	22
BC	—	1.4	98.6	18
All	3.6	3.6	92.8	251
Paper				
Br	26.8	6.2	67.0	16
BC	—	7.4	92.6	36
All	4.8	6.3	88.9	154
Engine				
Br	21.6	4.0	74.4	64
BC	—	1.4	98.6	15
All	8.6	3.6	87.8	150
Biscuit				
Br	16.8	11.2	72.0	74
BC	—	—	100.0	3
All	11.3	7.5	89.1	128
Rubber				
Br	23.2	4.4	72.4	51
BC	—	—	100.0	12
All	8.5	2.4	89.1	138
All factories				
Br	23.0	7.1	69.9	227
BC	—	2.7	97.3	84
All	5.4	4.0	90.6	821

Variations among factories in distribution of Brahmans, $X^2 = 27.18$, df = 10, p = .02.

Brahmans x all-castes in all other factories, $X^2 = 292.2$, df = 2, p < .01.

Backward Classes x all other castes in all factories, $X^2 = 36.83$, df = 2, p < .01.

Brahmans x Backward Classes, $X^2 = 154.61$, df = 2, p < .01.

clerks from the Backward Classes, and, except for the paper factory (7.4 per cent), less than 3 per cent of the Backward Classes are supervisors.

At the extremes of the hierarchy, then, caste is associated with occupational class. Between these two extremes, no stable relationship appears in the data. We may now turn to the question of whether, as in the case of education and literacy in English, caste and ethnic group affiliation tend to sort workers into the occupational classes, but become largely irrelevant within the classes. There are not enough non-Brahman castes represented to make feasible a general caste comparison among the supervisors and clerks, so that within these two classes a simple Brahman, non-Brahman division will be used.

Within the factories there are generally at least two distinct classes of supervisors. In the newer factories there is first a class of superior overseers, department heads, and general technicians such as engineers and chemists, who lie mid-way between the managerial staff and the next class of supervisors who are responsible for and deal directly with the workers. The superior supervisor is paid considerably more and has much higher prestige than those dealing directly with the men. In the engine factory, 3 out of the 4 superior supervisors who appeared in the sample were Brahmans, and in both the biscuit and rubber factories 2 out of 3 were Brahmans. In the textile mill, the gap occurs between the jobbers who oversee the actual production and supervisors above the jobber level. Ten out of the 15 Brahman supervisors in the textile mill are above the jobber level and only two workers from other castes, one a CKP and one a Shimpi, fall in the same category. In the paper mill, the prestige ranking runs from supervisor at the top, then foreman, then assistant foreman. There are three Brahmans at the supervisor level, one at the foreman level, and none among the assistant foremen.

The Brahman supremacy within the ranks of the supervisors is also found among the clerks. Since the clerical sub-divisions are not so clear-cut as those among the supervisors, average wages have been used as a basis for comparison. It will be seen from Table LXI that in every factory the Brahmans receive significantly higher mean wages than the other castes.

TABLE LXI

MEAN MONTHLY WAGE OF BRAHMANS AND OTHER ETHNIC
GROUPS AMONG CLERICAL WORKERS, BY FACTORY

	Brahmans		Other Groups	
	Number in Sample	Mean Monthly Wage Rs.	Number in Sample	Mean Monthly Wage Rs.
Textile	3	201.4	6	148.5
Paper	3	173.7	2	122.0
Engine	23	182.7	2	135.0
Biscuit	15	140.7	3	106.7
Rubber	19	123.2	4	101.0

In brief, then, in the two highest occupational classes, the supervisors and clerks, the Brahmans are not only most heavily represented numerically, but they tend to hold the highest ranking positions.

Below the supervisory and clerical group, among the laborers the position is much less clear. Table LXII tests the general hypothesis that in each factory ethnic groups differ significantly in their status within the permanent P & M worker category. The F score given at the bottom of each column is a measure of whether or not the variations in average work among the different ethnic categories are sufficient to state that they are not chance sampling variations.

None of the five F scores is significant, so that all the fluctuations in mean current monthly wage fall within the

TABLE LXII

MEAN CURRENT MONTHLY WAGE IN RUPEES FOR ETHNIC
CATEGORIES AMONG PERMANENT P & M WORKERS

Ethnic Category	Textile	Paper	Engine	Biscuit	Rubber
Brahmans	93.3	113.6	99.4	61.5	82.2
Marathas	93.2	77.5	88.3	67.8	72.8
Intermediate	89.5	85.6	91.4	77.5	78.6
Village artisans	99.1	70.0	138.6	60.0	66.7
Village servants	102.8	88.9	61.0	56.7	72.5
Backward castes	86.2	83.8	78.6	60.9	77.5
Other regions	102.5	80.0	83.4	80.8	71.2
Other religions	87.2	97.5	105.9	68.6	70.0
All castes	93.8	85.3	93.1	66.7	77.1
F score	1.23	0.57	3.35	1.24	1.76

limits which could have occurred by chance and the data do not support the hypothesis. It is possible, however, that mean wage differences among ethnic categories, while not significant within a factory, do follow roughly the same order from one plant to another. To test this hypothesis, the mean scores for each factory were ranked and, by use of Kendall's Coefficient of Concordance (W), the consistency of the rankings among the five factories was tested. The matrix of ranks is given below.

The results of this test show that any agreement among factories in the rank order of mean wages of ethnic groups was as likely as not to have occurred by chance, again leading to the conclusion that no over-all relationship between castes and wages appears among the P & M workers.

While no over-all relationship appears, it is possible that the social ranking system in the general society does operate at the two extremes of the hierarchy, while the intermediate rankings are not reflected in differential

TABLE LXIII

RANK ORDER OF ETHNIC CATEGORIES WITHIN FACTORIES
RANKED BY MEAN CURRENT MONTHLY WAGE

Ethnic Category	Textile	Paper	Engine	Biscuit	Rubber
Brahmans	4	1	3	1	5
Marathas	5	7	5	4	4
Intermediate	6	4	4	2	2
Village artisans	3	8	1	8	7
Village servants	1	3	8	5	8
Backward castes	8	5	7	3	6
Other regions	2	6	6	6	1
Other religions	7	2	2	7	3

W = 0.16, p > .50

rankings within the factory. As in the case of the supervisors and clerks, the top of the hierarchy, the Brahmans
will be considered separately. The Backward Classes, who
were too rarely represented in the clerical and supervisory
classes to have any general ranking within these groups,
are also treated separately in the following discussion.

The Brahman's clear superiority among the clerical and
supervisory personnel is not so evident among the P & M
workers. Only in the paper and biscuit factories do they
receive significantly higher wages.

TABLE LXIV

MEAN CURRENT MONTHLY WAGES IN RUPEES FOR BRAHMANS AND
NON-BRAHMANS AMONG PERMANENT P & M WORKERS,
BY FACTORY

Factory	Brahmans	Others	All Groups
Textile	93.3	93.8	93.8
Paper	113.6*	83.0	85.3
Engine	99.4	93.0	95.0
Biscuit	82.2*	73.3	77.1
Rubber	61.5	68.6	66.7

* Significantly higher at p < .05.

159

In the biscuit factory, the higher average wage is a result of the absence of Brahmans at the very lowest wage and skill levels. In the paper mill, the Brahmans do occupy a special position. None of the Brahmans is engaged in the manufacturing process itself. The Brahmans at the P & M worker level included a dispensary dresser, a watchman, finishers, and ream binders. The last two occupations, exclusively filled by Brahmans imported from Uttar Pradesh, are interesting in that they are "white collar" by comparison with other laboring jobs in the factory. In fact, the finishing room where these occupations are carried on is separated from the other operations and is airier and cleaner.

In the other factories the Brahmans among P & M workers do not earn appreciably higher salaries; in fact, in two out of three, their wages are lower than the mean current monthly wage of the other castes.

At the other end of the caste continuum the position of the Harijans and other Backward Classes is clearer. In our sample, there are no Harijans among the clerks in any factory. They are occasionally represented among the supervisors. There are none among the supervisors of the biscuit or rubber factories. In the textile mill, out of 84 supervisors there are two Mahars, and one who reported himself simply as "Harijan." In the engine factory there is one Harijan out of 22 supervisors. Only in the paper mill do they have any appreciable representation. There are 6 Mahars, 1 Cambhar, and 3 who call themselves Harijans, or a total of 10 out of 38 foremen and supervisors. The heavy representation in the paper mill is a remnant of an earlier labor system in which the mill contracted with a nearby "criminal tribe" compound for a large portion of its least skilled labor, and this company is the only one of

160

the five with any significant numbers of so-called "tribals," mostly Vadars and Kaikadis.

At the P & M worker level, the Backward Classes are either too few in number for comparison, as in the biscuit factory where there are only two in the entire plant, or lower in mean current monthly wages than other caste groups.

TABLE LXV

Mean Current Wages of Backward Classes and Other Ethnic Groups Among Permanent P & M Workers, by Factory

	Backward Classes	All Others	
Factory	Rs.	Rs.	C.R.[a]
Textile	86.0	94.5	2.28
Paper	83.8	85.9	0.20
Engine	78.6	97.6	2.95
Biscuit[b]	—	—	—
Rubber	60.9	67.5	2.18

[a] C.R. is the critical ratio of the difference between the means. If it is greater than 1.96, the difference is significant at $p < .05$.

[b] Too few cases for comparison.

To recapitulate the findings on the reflection of ethnic grouping upon hierarchical position within the factories, the only substantial differences are for Brahmans and for Backward Classes. Brahmans are disproportionately represented in the clerical and supervisory classes and hold the highest ranking positions within those classes. Their relative position among the P & M workers depends upon the factory, and in most factories it is not substantially higher. The Backward Classes are hardly represented at all among the supervisors and clerks and are either absent or lower in mean wages in all factories. Aside from Brahmans and Backward Classes, the general ranking of castes does not seem to be reflected in significant differences in hierarchical positions within the factories.

Caste versus Education

So far we have dealt with caste and education separately, but the two are clearly correlated, as Table LXVI indicates.

TABLE LXVI

PERCENTAGE IN EACH EDUCATIONAL LEVEL BY ETHNIC CATEGORY
AMONG ALL WORKERS IN ALL FACTORIES

Ethnic Category	No Education	Primary	Secondary	Matriculate	College	Number in Sample
Brahman	1.6	10.6	53.1	27.9	6.8	228
Maratha	35.8	36.7	23.5	2.6	1.4	242
Intermediate	39.0	28.7	29.7	2.4	0.3	68
Village artisan	26.8	45.7	21.7	2.2	3.5	37
Village servant	37.0	34.1	28.2	—	0.7	44
Backward classes	62.1	21.0	15.9	—	1.0	84
Other regions	32.2	29.0	24.7	5.1	9.0	55
Other religions	24.0	44.4	28.2	2.9	0.5	57
All groups	25.4	24.8	34.0	9.8	6.0	815[a]

$X^2 = 1397.53$, df $= 35$, C $= .50$, p $< .01$.
[a] Six cases no information.

The Brahmans have by far the highest educational level of any of the ethnic categories, and the Backward Classes by far the lowest, but even removing these two, ethnic category shows a significant relationship ($X^2 = 133.07$, df $= 15$, p $< .01$, C $= 0.20$).[3]

---

[3] Even with their educational superiority in the factory, the Brahmans in the factory population are significantly lower in educational level than the Brahmans in the adult male population in Poona. The educational distribution of the Brahmans in the factory was compared with the adult male non-educands in the Poona Resurvey (Table 1.11 p. 42), $X^2 = 108.66$, df $= 4$, p $< .01$, while the Backward Classes in the factories have the same low educational level as they have in the general population.

While caste, particularly Brahman versus non-Brahman status, and high or low education are at present coinciding attributes of each individual, because of the theoretical importance of the ascribed versus achieved status distinction, it is nevertheless important to attempt to separate the effect of the two variables. Conceivably, the educational distribution among the ethnic categories may change at some future date, and it is important to note whether on present evidence it is the amount of education or the ethnic category which is the prime ranking variable. Since we will be dealing with the combined factory population for these tests, we must first examine the way in which both education and caste pay off in the factory hierarchies taken jointly, rather than separately. For this purpose, the mean current wage of each educational group and each caste or ethnic group is given in Tables LXVII and LXVIII.

TABLE LXVII

MEAN CURRENT MONTHLY WAGE OF EDUCATIONAL
CLASSES IN ALL FACTORIES

	Number in Sample	Mean Monthly Wage in Rs.
No Education	207	90.0
Up to Primary	202	90.6
Post-primary non-matriculate	277	98.7
Matriculate	129	174.5

$F = 68.80$, $p < .01$.
Six cases omitted for lack of relevant data.

Educational level clearly influences the wage level of the workers. It becomes an important factor, however, only when the worker has more education than just primary schooling, and therefore in most tables in this chapter those

163

with only primary education will be combined with the workers who have had no education at all.

TABLE LXVIII

MEAN WAGE OF ALL WORKERS BY ETHNIC GROUP
IN ALL FACTORIES COMBINED

Ethnic Group	Number in Sample	Mean Monthly Wage in Rs.
Brahman	228	128.88
Maratha	242	95.32
Intermediate	68	97.39
Village artisan	37	114.30
Village servant	44	82.22
Backward classes	84	88.02
Other region	55	115.64
Other religion	57	101.84

$F = 0.73$, $p > .05$.
Six cases omitted for lack of relevant data.

It is clear from this table that the Brahmans rank highest in wages—they are in fact significantly higher than all the other groups combined (C. R. = 5.27, $p < .01$) —but there is no over-all significant relationship between wages and ethnic group. The Backward Classes are not the lowest group, surpassing the Village Servant, but this is a statistical artifact of the dispersion of Backward Classes throughout the occupational range in a single factory, the paper mill.

To analyze the more general question of the relative importance of caste and education, we held one variable at a time constant and computed the mean wage differences in the other one. Table LXIX shows the mean wage of each caste within the different educational levels.

Even the Brahman superiority evident in the other tables disappears when they are compared with other

TABLE LXIX

MEAN WAGE OF EACH CASTE BY EDUCATIONAL LEVEL

	No Education		Primary		Non-Matriculate		Matriculate	
	Number in Sample	Mean Rs. Wage	Number in Sample	Mean Rs. Wage	Number in Sample	Mean Rs. Wage	Number in Sample	Mean Rs. Wage
Brahman	2	90.0	19	86.0	115	95.6	92	180.2
Maratha	86	95.0	82	92.1	64	101.3	10	86.4
Intermediate	24	90.3	18	92.4	22	105.3	4	118.8
Village artisan	8	103.1	10	92.2	14	105.5	5	201.6
Village servant	16	85.0	16	90.5	11	92.7	1	90.0
Backward classes	44	81.4	24	94.8	15	98.0	1	70.0
Other regions	15	87.6	14	85.3	15	109.5	11	200.9
Other religions	12	87.1	19	85.0	21	91.8	5	243.4
All groups	207	90.0	202	90.6	227	98.7	129	174.5
F score		1.13		2.65		1.07		1.34

castes and ethnic groups within their own educational class. Reading down the columns it will be noted that there is no consistent order among the ethnic groups in mean wage, nor are any of the F scores significant. From this we may conclude that when educational level is held constant, caste or ethnic category is not a basis of preferential ranking within the factory hierarchy.

Reading across the rows, we see that the mean wage for each ethnic category increases as education increases, but there are enough exceptions to the pattern to call for a closer look. Two further tests were made. The educational differences were dichotomized into primary and below, and secondary or higher. Here all the differences are in the proper direction and statistically significant.

The data were also broken down by factories. It was anticipated that the higher the educational group within each caste and factory, the higher the mean wage would be. Fifty-three out of the 65, or 81.5 per cent of the sequences followed the proper pattern. If education were not a ranking variable independent of caste, the ranking of mean wages by educational group within the caste should occur at random, and 50 per cent of the sequences should have been in error.

The data indicate that education, not caste, is the primary ranking variable when they are statistically separated. We must remember, however, that these two variables are not in fact separate. If they did get much further out of line than they are now, it is possible that their relative importance might change.

Workers' Perceptions of Caste Relevance

In view of these findings, it is interesting to find out whether the workers see caste as an important element in their career chances. To test the workers' own perceptions, we first asked whether they believed they would have had a better chance for advancement if they belonged to another caste. Almost half the workers, 44.7 per cent, believed that it would have helped. The proportions in each company were remarkably similar; the total range was only about 3 per cent. This close similarity among companies enabled us to combine the individual samples into one unit to determine the nature of the preferences. That is to say, what is the prized ethnic group for each caste. Table LXX gives the percentage of workers in each ethnic group that thought that no other caste affiliation would have helped them, and the percentage who thought belonging to the Brahman, Maratha, Harijan castes, or coming from another region, or subscribing to another religion, would have assisted their careers. The gradations from intermediate castes through backward tribes was omitted because no one mentioned these as desirable caste affiliations.

TABLE LXX

Caste Preference for Advancement by Worker's Own Caste

Worker's Caste	Caste Preference							
	None	Brahman	Maratha	Harijan	Other Region	Other Religion	Don't Know	Total Number[b]
Brahman	63.2	—	8.3	14.0	4.8	.4	14.9	228
Maratha	54.1	25.2	—	2.1	10.3	.4	15.7	242
Intermediate	55.9	27.9	1.5	2.9	8.8	—	11.8	68
Village artisan	43.2	16.2	—	5.4	21.6	5.4	21.6	37
Village servant	58.1	25.6	2.3	2.3	9.3	—	11.6	43
Backward tribes	58.3	16.7	8.3	—	8.3	—	8.3	12
Harijan	45.8	38.9	9.7	—	8.3	2.8	12.5	72
Other region	54.2	25.4	8.5	—	—	1.7	20.3	58
Other religion	45.8	35.6	1.7	3.4	15.3	—	11.9	59
No information	50.0	—	—	—	—	—	50.0	22
All castes	55.3	27.5[a]	6.0[a]	5.9[a]	9.2[a]	1.0[a]	15.0	821

[a] Percentage of members of other castes mentioning this caste.
[b] Multiple choices were allowed, so percentage totals may exceed 100 per cent.

The first fact that strikes one from a perusal of the table is that the proportion of workers satisfied with their caste is, except for the Brahmans, relatively constant at about half. One might reasonably have expected the percentages of other-caste oriented workers to have increased as the worker's position in the caste hierarchy declined. The Brahmans are clearly and understandably the most satisfied with their own caste affiliation, and they are by far the group

most commonly envied by the other groups. What is surprising is that the percentages do not reflect a more re-
sounding victory. Less than two-thirds of the Brahmans are
certain that their caste affiliation is strategically the best,
and only about one-fourth of the workers feel that being a
Brahman would help them. Brahman-envy is highest among
the Harijans and among the advocates of other religions, in
part because this category contains some Buddhists, who
in other times would have called themselves Harijans.

The most surprising figures in the table are the 5.9 per
cent of all other castes who feel that Harijan status would
have helped them and the 14 per cent of the Brahmans who
responded in this way. It is difficult to know exactly what
this means. Whether it is a general reaction to the special
prerogatives of Harijans is difficult to say, but it does not
appear to be likely in view of our earlier finding of the
genuinely lower skill and wage rankings of the Harijans in
the factories. It does not appear to be inaccurate reporting
in that the percentages largely held up under re-interview-
ing. The relatively high percentage of Brahmans who gave
this response makes it even more puzzling. Aside from the
detailed percentages, however, the hard fact to emerge
from Table LXX is that about half the workers in each
ethnic category feel that they were hampered by their
ethnic affiliation, and that their other caste aspirations are
more complicated than a simple prediction on the basis of
caste hierarchy would indicate.

Educational Aspirations

Even with the relatively high importance they gave to
caste, the workers were not eager to neglect the acquisition
of the chief achieved-status attribute, education. While the
workers were not asked their judgment of this criteria as a

status ranking variable within the factory, they were asked about their own hypothetical educational aspirations and, to give their imagination freer rein, how much education they would want their sons to have if they could afford it. Educational aspirations emerge much more clearly than do occupational aspirations. Only 5.0 per cent of the workers were satisfied with their own education attainments, and fewer still (3.2 per cent) wanted their sons to have the same amount of education as they had had. No one aspired to less education either for himself or his son. In general, educational aspirations for the workers' sons were higher than for themselves at all levels of education. For the sons, the most common aspiration was for the matriculate level, equivalent to high school graduation in the West. Only 5.5 per cent of all workers wanted less than matriculate status for their sons. Educational aspirations were directly related to the workers' own education, the lower the worker's educational attainments the lower his aspiration both for himself and his son, but even with this in mind the aspirations were high. Only 12.2 per cent of those with no education wished their sons to have less than matriculate status, compared with the general average of 5.5 per cent for all workers. Two-thirds of the workers with some middle school training wanted some college education for their sons, compared with 28.7 per cent of those who had no education. The point where more than half the workers wanted college training for themselves was at the secondary school level, while more than half the workers who had had middle school training wanted a college education for their sons. It is clear that any limitation on the expansion in educational attainments does not lie in lack of aspirations. It is also clear that the aspiration did not produce current action in that none of the workers in the sample was enrolled in a school at the time of the study.

Work Experience and Factory Status

We have so far discussed the correlation between occupational category or wage level and social characteristics whose origin and primary frame of reference are external to the factory. We can now turn to the worker's occupational history, which should, in an ideal-typical factory system, be the major if not the sole determinant of current status. We should have some measure of the efficiency and productivity of the worker's past and present job performance, but no way was devised to measure these important variables in a questionnaire study of this type. We do have some data reflecting the kind and amount of work experience of each worker both prior and subsequent to his entry into the present factory.

Previous Work Experience

The first question we ask is whether the top P & M positions in each factory tend to be filled by people who come to the factory with some experience, or conversely whether imported skills are differentially rewarded in the wage hierarchy. Table LXXI answers these questions by giving for each factory the mean wages of P & M workers with three different levels of external experience as compared with P & M workers without such experience.

Only the figures marked with a superscript "b" indicate a statistically significant difference. As might be expected, in none of the factories are workers with any of the levels of experience paid significantly less than the inexperienced. However, the differential rewards of experience vary from one factory to another. While we were dealing with ex-

TABLE LXXI

Types of Experience and Differences in Mean Wage, in Rupees, Between Experienced and Inexperienced Laborers, by Factory

	Any Previous Job		Previous Factory Job		Previous Job in Entry	
	Per Cent With Experience	Diff.[a] in Mean Wage	Per Cent With Experience	Diff.[a] in Mean Wage	Per Cent With Experience	Diff.[a] in Mean Wage
Textile	71.65	− 1.54	50.39	+ 0.88	37.80	+ 5.21[b]
Paper	34.41	− 2.82	24.73	− 1.84	9.68	+14.68
Engine	59.77	+13.26[b]	44.83	+19.53[b]	32.18	+19.01[b]
Biscuit	64.10	− 3.36	47.44	− 2.44	26.92	+ 1.08
Rubber	46.67	+12.88[b]	24.44	+21.66[b]	16.67	+17.03[b]

[a] Difference computed by subtracting the mean current wage of group with no prior experience of the type specified from the mean current wage of the group with such experience.
[b] Significant difference between means at $p < .05$ level.

ternally-based social characteristics, the most efficient typology for distinguishing different systems of rewards was the new versus the old factory division. Now that we come to work experience proper, this typology no longer accounts for different patterns and we must turn to our production system typology. Except for the special case of the rubber factory, the Type A factories—paper and biscuit—gave no special advantage to any previous experience. This, of course, is what we would anticipate in view of their relatively simple skill structure and absence of genuinely transferable skills. The apparent high reward given to previous experience in the rubber factory is a result of its exaggerated slab-like structure, so that a few imported skilled workers are sharply set off from the mass of workers receiving unskilled wages. This situation is the result of a very recent change in the complexity of the manufacturing process, which required the external recruitment of a number of highly skilled workers. It is unlikely that this striking advantage will continue.

171

More interesting is the contrast between the Type B and the Type C factories. The textile mill rewards only previous experience directly related to the job for which the worker was employed, showing the highly specific form of skill used in the pigeonhole-like structure of the mill. The more fluid engine factory rewarded all kinds of previous experience, since it was engaged in its own training and socialization process. The generalized value of experience lay both in the socialization of the worker to employment and the factory and his general familiarity with machines that he is called upon to direct, not just tend. Part of this skill, in any case, will be learned inside the factory, but previous experience serves as a "leg-up" in the process.

Seniority in the Present Company

While we do not have data on the worker's performance in his present job, we can approach the question indirectly through the correlation between seniority and wages. To the extent that seniority is the primary determinant of wage differences, we might conceive of the factory following a model where workers would enter the factory at the bottom of the wage hierarchy, gradually acquire skills and, either through the expansion of the factory or the retirement of older workers, move up the occupational and wage ladders. The factories might then differ in the slope of the regression line and the intercepts— that is, in the degree of wage differentiation, the general wage level, and the rapidity with which the workers move up the ladder; but the correlations would be the same. To the extent that other variables intrude, such as the external recruitment of higher level skills or other criteria for promotion than seniority, the correlation would decline. Table LXXII gives the seniority distribution, the mean wage for each seniority group among P & M

172

TABLE LXXII

Seniority Distributions, Mean Wage for Each Seniority Group Among Permanent P & M Workers, and the Correlation Between Current Wages and Seniority, by Factory

Years Seniority	Textile		Paper		Engine		Biscuit		Rubber	
	Per Cent of Total N=127	Mean Wage Rs.	Per Cent of Total N=93	Mean Wage Rs.	Per Cent of Total N=87	Mean Wage Rs.	Per Cent of Total	Mean Wage Rs.	Per Cent of Total N=90	Mean Wage Rs.
1-2	2.36	79.00	2.15	108.50	17.24	71.93	3.85	66.67	55.56	67.60
3-4	0.79	100.00	7.53	75.43	20.69	86.00	5.13	77.25	16.67	60.40
5-6	8.66	95.55	1.08	66.00	17.24	90.80	5.13	70.50	10.00	66.89
7-8	16.54	97.29	12.90	81.67	44.83	105.33	20.51	68.19	7.78	70.29
9-10	15.75	88.95	6.45	82.83	—	—	8.97	70.71	2.22	63.00
11-15	30.71	94.08	31.18	83.21	—	—	47.44	78.57	7.78	70.43
16-20	15.75	90.55	17.20	89.25	—	—	2.56	101.00	—	—
21-25	4.72	95.00	6.45	90.00	—	—	3.85	96.67	—	—
26-30	3.94	102.00	8.60	97.38	—	—	2.56	117.50	—	—
30+	0.79	80.00	6.45	80.83	—	—	—	—	—	—
Mean	yrs. 10.6	Rs. 93.84	yrs. 14.7	Rs. 85.30	yrs. 5.1	Rs. 93.07	yrs. 9.4	Rs. 77.06	yrs. 3.9	Rs. 66.68
	r = +.38[a]		r = +.08		r = +.55[a]		r = +.77[a]		r = −0.74[a]	

[a] Significant correlations, p < .01.

workers, and the Pearsonian coefficient of correlation for each factory.

From the table, it can be seen that the relationship between wages and seniority, where it does exist, is a much more complex one than the model would permit. Moreover, while differences in the rewards given to previous experience tend to coincide with our production process typology, variations in the correlation between wages and seniority do not. Rather, they seem to flow from idiosyncratic features peculiar to the history and current organization of each company. In three out of the five factories there was a significant positive correlation between wages and seniority, in one no correlation was apparent, and in the last a strong negative correlation was found. Only in the engine and the biscuit factories was the correlation high enough to approximate our simple model, and then for very different reasons.

The strong negative correlation in the rubber factory was a by-product of the recent change in the manufacturing process referred to earlier, which required the employment of a few skilled workers from outside who all fall in the one to two year category. The narrow range of salaries of the other workers, referred to in Chapter IV, gave these recent additions to the workforce undue weight. A look at the distribution of means by seniority groups, which, under our model should show a steady increase in magnitude, indicates clearly the haphazard relationship between seniority and wages in this firm. There was no system of periodic wage increments in this firm and, with more than half of the employees having less than three years seniority, no reflection of upward mobility as yet appeared in the wage hierarchy.

The paper factory, which showed no over-all correlation between wages and seniority, did, upon examination of the line of means, appear to be a more orderly progression. The weakness in the over-all correlation was primarily a result of the existence of a very stable, low-skill group that remained with the factory for long periods of time at low wages. For example, twenty-two women whose job was to pick and sort waste paper and carry bundles on their heads, remained at this low skill level no matter how long they stayed with the company. Without them, the correlation is + .17, which is statistically significant, as compared with + .08 for the full group. Similarly, a number of men in the unskilled category with 20 to 30 years seniority disturbed the wage-seniority relationship. Conversely, what turnover did take place occurred above this skill level.

Among the three firms that did show a significant, positive over-all correlation, different factors seem to have been operating. Since the textile mill was just one unit in an extended industrial complex, the number of people moving into a job from outside tended to be equal or greater than the number recruited from below. With no system of seniority raises and with wages geared to industry-wide rates for specific jobs, a correlation between seniority and wages reflects differential turnover at the various skill levels. Where, in this case, the correlation is positive, it reflects a lower turnover at the upper skill levels. The variations among the means did not progress in an orderly fashion, giving evidence of the operation of strong chance factors in the recruitment and departure of personnel at various levels over the years.

The biscuit and engine factories were much more regular in the relationship between seniority and wages, but again for slightly different reasons. In the biscuit factory, the range of skills was very narrow, and most increases in salary resulted from periodic wage increases. Moreover, the gradual mechanization of the plant, accompanied by a decline in total workers from 216 in 1950 to 129 in 1956, weeded out many of the lower-ranking workers. The few replacements were brought in at the lower pay scales.

It was the engine factory, with its rapid expansion and wide range of skills, that most clearly approximated the ideal pattern. Both a strong positive correlation and the regular step-like progression of the class means were results of the relatively high and uniform rate of upward mobility of workers as they remained with the company. Turnover was extremely low, and as the company expanded, it tended to train its own skilled workers.

We have examined the extent to which seniority determined wage differentials in each factory and in general concluded that the degree of correlation in most of the factories depended upon differential turnover rates, the tendency toward external recruitment of skills versus internal training and promotion, and upon the over-all dimensions of the skill structure.

Given the limited skill level and importation of skills from the outside, in these factories it is conceivable, but not likely, that the longer the worker stays in the factory, the better is his job performance. It is more likely that, after an initial apprenticeship period, seniority is a variable only loosely associated with productivity. Do the workers think that seniority rather than job performance should be the primary basis for promotion? Each worker was asked whether he believed that seniority (kāmgār kitī varṣha kāmgār āhe) or job performance (kāmgār kitī cãgle kām karto) should be the paramount consideration. As indicated in Table LXXIII, the overwhelming answer to this question was job performance.

Aside from the over-all preference for performance over

176

TABLE LXXIII

CHOICE OF MOST IMPORTANT FACTOR IN PROMOTION
AMONG ALL WORKERS, BY FACTORY
(PER CENT)

Factor	Textile	Paper	Engine	Biscuit	Rubber	All Factories
Seniority	25.1	35.4	10.1	13.9	14.0	22.6
Performance	74.9	64.6	89.9	86.1	86.0	77.4
No. workers	2342	603	614	159	531	4249

$X^2 = 131.39$, df = 4, p $<$ .01.

seniority, the differences among the factories are considerable. The workers in the engine factory are almost unani-
mous in their preference for job performance, while more
than a third of the workers in the paper factory prefer
seniority. We immediately note that the paper factory
workers had the highest mean seniority of any of the
factories.

One might first ask whether the proportion of workers
choosing seniority is correlated with the degree of association between wages and seniority in the different factories.
No such relationship is apparent. If anything, there is a
possible negative relationship, with the seniority-preferring
paper mill employees working in a factory where there is
almost no correlation between wages and seniority, while
the biscuit factory, with its high correlation, has a low
proportion of workers wanting seniority to be the primary
determinant of promotion. Nor do the differences among
factories in the proportion of seniority-preferring workers
coincide with our production process typology. The most
efficient classification, in fact, seems to be our division
between the older factories (paper and textile mills) and
the newer factories (engine, biscuit, and rubber factories).

177

This would lead one to suspect that the differences among the companies are the result of the fact that few workers in the newer factories have attained very much seniority and that those who favor seniority are the workers who are themselves senior. This is in fact so. Merging all of the workforces, we see that the average age of those choosing seniority is significantly higher than those choosing job performance, and in the two older companies a worker's own seniority is closely associated with his preference for seniority as the major factor in promotion. It remains to be seen whether the newer factories will reach this higher level of preference for seniority when their age structures deepen. The over-riding fact remains, however, that in all the factories, two-thirds or more of the workers prefer job performance. It is interesting to note that the greatest preference for seniority occurred in the one factory, the paper mill, where there was no correlation between seniority and current wage, so that the one factory where seniority as a basis for wage gradations would have been acceptable to a large proportion of the workers is the only one where the correlation does not obtain. We have no measure of job performance, but it is clear that relative importance of seniority seems contrary to the expressed wishes of the workers.

WORKERS' PSYCHOLOGICAL INVOLVEMENT

In the ideal-typical factory organization, there is a set of inter-linked structural and psychological features which serve to legitimize the status hierarchy and at the same time provide the primary motivation to maximal productivity among the workers. Structurally, the intra-factory status hierarchy should parallel differences in productivity and skill, or, from the viewpoint of the individual worker, his placement and promotion chances should derive from these work-relevant attributes. We have noted that many of the variables related to hierarchical position, as measured by occupational class, skill grade, and current wage, are not particularly relevant to productivity. Only in the Type C factory does it appear that the hierarchical structure might correlate well with individual productivity differences. Psychologically, the ideal-typical factory organization calls for the involvement of the worker in the pursuit of ever higher intra-factory status. This involvement should be both to the general notion of advancement as a meaningful life goal and to the specific pursuit of increased status within the factory in which the worker now finds himself.

We have already reflected somewhat on the general mobility orientation and its link to productivity. We argued in Chapter III that most of the workers were interested in acquiring "permanent" property rights in a job and that this carries with it a notion of minimal quality of performance but not an internalized drive for continuously enhanced productivity. Moreover, we noted on several occasions the workers' belief that the most important variable affecting career enhancement is influence. Moreover, the general impression one gets in reading the literature on Indian factory laborers and in talking with factory managers is that a factory job is a form of property to the worker and that he will seek to retain, but not improve it. Gradations within the factory hierarchy seem to have very little meaning outside the compound, and, in general, the worker's status in the general society seems not to be increased by upward occupational mobility within the factory. There are, of course, exceptions to this general statement. Movement into the supervisory level is a meaningful "caste" move, and, as we shall see, is the most important component of workers' inter-class occupational mobility aspirations. Possibly, movement into an artisan occupation such as mason or wireman might be important to the worker and his family, but we have seen that few of these workers are recruited from within the factory. Also, if vertical mobility were to express itself in conspicuously increased consumption, promotion would have status-enhancing properties in the broader society. However, we have already seen that wage increases tend to be absorbed by increased dependency loads in the family, so that standards of living do not radically shift with upward occupational mobility within the factory. All of this would lead us to expect the workers to place a relatively low emphasis on occupational mobility, and a relatively heavy emphasis upon retention of the job. The security drive would be made even more pressing by the general abundance of labor and by the difficulties encountered in passing through the non-permanent segment of the factory workforce.

To test this general formulation, we asked the workers to make a choice among three possible jobs: one that provided security, but low pay and little chance for advancement; one that was insecure and had little possibility for upward mobility, but paid high wages; and one that was less secure, had low current wages, but promised future improvement in occupational position. We anticipated that job security would be the most common choice. Whether wage or occupational level aspirations would have the most attraction was an open question. Table LXXIV indicates the nature of the choices, by factory.

First, it can be seen that in all companies the majority of workers chose security, but the proportion is not out of line with those found in other countries, and the margin varies

TABLE LXXIV

CHARACTERISTICS MOST SOUGHT IN CHOOSING JOB,
ALL WORKERS, BY FACTORY
(PER CENT)

Characteristic	Textile	Paper	Engine	Biscuit	Rubber	All Factories
Guaranteed permanent	59.3	60.8	53.7	65.7	54.3	58.3
Higher pay	16.4	12.4	6.6	11.2	15.3	14.1
Advancement	22.5	26.5	38.8	22.4	29.9	26.4
No response	1.8	—	0.9	0.6	0.5	1.2
No. workers	2342	603	614	159	531	4249

among the companies.[4] The engine factory has the highest
percentage of workers who would choose upward mobility,
and the workers in the factory who were lowest in both
forms of aspiration are also the most security-seeking.
While the hypothesis concerning the primacy of the
security motive is corroborated, the differences among the
factories in the relative attraction of wage increases and
occupational advancement are interesting. For the combined factory workforce, advancement wins out with an
advantage of a little less than two to one. This ratio holds
true for the Type A factories where the absence of upper
level jobs does in fact restrict the upward mobility possibilities of the worker. It does not hold true for the Type
C engine factory and Type B textile mill that have more
dispersed skill structures. In the engine factory, with its
high mobility rate and high aspiration levels, the choice is

[4] For a review of the relative importance of security, wages and
advancement in Western factories, see Morris S. Viteles, *Motivation
and Morale in Industry*, New York: W. W. Norton, Inc., 1953, Ch.
16, "The Need for Security." The evidence of the various studies is
conflicting, but the general sense of them supports the primacy of
security.

181

clearly for a job with a chance for occupational advancement. In the textile mill, with its pigeonhole-like structure with little vertical mobility and low aspiration levels, the attraction of higher pay is stronger.

It would appear likely that the worker's position in the occupational and wage hierarchies would influence his preference for security, higher pay, or chance for advancement. To examine this relationship, we made a number of comparisons. First it was hypothesized that non-permanent workers would give higher priority to security. In none of the factories did a significantly higher proportion of non-permanent workers choose security. In fact, in four out of the five factories a lower proportion elected security, although the differences were not statistically significant. Second, it was anticipated that the supervisors, having had some taste of advancement, would prefer this to security. In all the factories a lower percentage of supervisors chose security and a higher percentage chose occupational advancement. It was also hypothesized that among the laborers the search for security would be negatively associated with wage level. There were no significant differences in mean current wage among laborers in any of the factories between those selecting the three alternatives. Differences between clerks and laborers or clerks and supervisors showed no consistent pattern. Except for the differences in preference among the supervisors, then, none of the anticipated relationships appeared. Therefore, the major discriminating variable seems to be which factory the worker is in, and not his position within the factory.

The ideal-typical factory organization calls not only for the linking of hierarchical position to productivity, which, as we have seen, is at best equivocal in the factories; and the general psychological involvement of the workers in the desire for upward mobility—which we have just seen—takes second place to security in most factories; but the development of the notion on the part of the individual worker that he personally has an opportunity for upward mobility in the factory in which he is currently employed. We shall examine this proposition on the basis of the responses to two questions each worker was asked: "In the factory in which you are now a worker, if you have good luck (daiv anukūl), what is the highest position you can get?" and "what is the highest monthly wage you expect to receive?" Table LXXV indicates in rough categories the absolute level of the hoped-for high working career wage, the mean difference between the wage level aspired to and the current wage for each P & M worker, and the mean difference expressed as a percentage of the current mean wage for permanent P & M workers.

If we look at the mean increase row, the high aspiration level of the Type C engine factory stands out (more than half the workers expect an increase of Rs. 80 or more), as does the low level of the paper mill, but aside from this the differences among the factories do not coincide with either our new versus old or production system typology. If, however, we compare the absolute wage aspirations with the current wage level (the last row), the newer factories—engine, biscuit and rubber—all have considerably higher aspiration levels than do the older paper and textile mills. It appears from these data that wage aspirations are related to the social characteristics of the workers in a factory and not primarily to the nature of the production system or the general structure of the skill hierarchy. The two highest absolute and relative wage aspirations occur in the factories with the highest and lowest mean current wages, and in the pyramidal Type C

183

TABLE LXXV

DIFFERENCE BETWEEN ASPIRED LIFE MONTHLY WAGE AND CURRENT
MONTHLY WAGE AMONG P & M WORKERS, BY FACTORY

	Per Cent of All Workers					
Rs. Increase	Textile	Paper	Engine	Biscuit	Rubber	All Factories
None	29.1	37.5	17.9	37.4	22.4	28.2
1-79	49.3	42.0	29.1	35.0	41.3	43.8
80 and over	21.6	20.5	53.0	27.6	36.3	28.0
Number of workers	2342	603	614	159	531	4249
Mean increase (Rs.)	60.41	34.95	86.85	62.11	66.40	75.65
Mean current wage (Rs.)	93.84	85.30	93.07	77.06	66.68	
Relative increase (%)[a]	63.8	40.1	96.7	80.6	99.6	

[a] Mean current wage divided into the mean increase.

factory, and the flattest of the slab-like Type A structures —the engine and rubber factories.

While wage aspirations give a fair indication of one division of general lifetime aspirations, we noted earlier that wages are a somewhat imperfect guide to hierarchical position within a factory. To focus specifically upon the problem of hierarchical aspirations within the factory structure, we must turn to the occupational grades, and the question concerning the highest position a P & M worker aspired to. The percentages of workers who aspire to become supervisors and to higher non-supervisory jobs are given for each factory in Table LXXVI.

The weighted average for all factories indicates that a little less than two-thirds of the P & M workers expect to remain at exactly the same rank so long as they stay in the present factory, and only about one-fourth of them think they have a chance of becoming supervisors. Clearly,

TABLE LXXVI

Aspirations of P & M Workers, by Factory
(Per Cent)

Aspiration Level	Textile	Paper	Engine	Biscuit	Rubber	All Factories
Supervisor	25.3	16.2	35.9	16.3	19.6	24.4
Higher P & M rank	12.0	21.6	16.5	3.1	6.8	13.2
Same rank	62.7	62.2	47.6	80.6	73.5	62.4
Sample size	158	111	103	98	102	3850

the bulk of the workers are "fatalistic," at least so far as upward mobility in their factories is concerned. But are there more optimists than the number of positions would warrant? Comparisons are complicated by the cumulative rather than the simultaneous occurrence of opportunities and by the age structure and possible expansion of the factories. The most reasonable comparisons can be made in terms of those who hope to move across occupational class lines into the relatively fixed supervisor class. One-fourth of the workers aspiring to be supervisors is more than the number to whom the current distribution of supervisory posts would promise success. In all the factories there are 22.8 workers for every supervisor, while one out of four workers aspires to be a supervisor, or almost six times as many workers aspire to be supervisors as there are supervisory positions. This disproportion is even further increased by noting that over one-third (37.3 per cent) of all supervisors in these factories were brought in from the outside and never served as workers in the factories where they are currently employed, making nine times as many aspirers as there are supervisory jobs internally filled.

185

We cannot, of course, directly translate levels of aspiration into proportions of workers who aspire and who do not aspire to a higher occupational class. This dichotomy tells us only that some workers aspire and others do not, not how much affect is attached to the aspiration. We can, however, ask ourselves how each of these two groups compares with the current supervisors in their own factory. This partition of the workers into three groups (leaving aside the clerical workers as outside of the production process and mobility stream entirely) also points out a possibly erroneous implication of the estimate of over-optimism given above—that all workers would have an equal chance to become supervisors. A worker who sees in himself the same characteristics that distinguish the supervisors from most of the workers may be operating with less over-estimation of his chances than is a worker with none of the attributes that currently qualify supervisors.

The discussion that follows is an attempt to determine whether this process whereby the worker measures himself against a proto-supervisor type seems to operate or whether the aspirers are distributed at random throughout the worker population. It was hypothesized that three sets of attributes would count within any factory—that is, would enter into the proto-supervisor type. These were: (1) current position and experience within the present factory, (2) earlier work experience, and (3) qualities of the individual unrelated to the factory itself. The relative importance of the three categories of variables in each of the factories indicates the extent to which factors operating to determine mobility within the company were within the present factory itself, were outside the present factory

186

but within the industrial structure at large, or lay in the non-industrial stratification system of the society.

The variables collected in the present study that fall within the three categories are given in the left-hand stub of Table LXXVII, each variable arranged so that the theoretical expectation is that the highest value of the percentage or mean should fall among those who are already supervisors, next highest among those who aspire to become supervisors, and the lowest among those who do not aspire to become supervisors (non-aspirers). The superscript "a" indicates that the variable discriminates at the $p < .05$ level of significance between the aspirers and the non-aspirers.

It can be seen at a glance that the five factories differ greatly in the variables that do distinguish the aspirers from the non-aspirers, and that the differences now coincide with production process contrasts rather than the new versus old dichotomy. In the Type A companies none of the discriminating variables was within either the present factory or the past work experience of the employee. They were all non-factory attributes: age; education, as measured by the percentage who had completed more than four years of schooling; sex; and, in two out of the three, caste. Because of the simplicity of the productive process involving only two- or three-step processing of raw materials, the low skill requirements, the supervisors do not need skills so much as they do general prestige to enable them to control the people working under them most efficiently. In the other two factories, the picture is quite different. In Type B, the textile mill, the only variables which discriminate between aspirers and non-aspirers are whether or not they have had previous factory experience and more specifically whether or not they had a previous

187

TABLE LXXVII

Comparison of Supervisors, Workers Who Aspire To Be Supervisors, and Non-Aspirers, by Mobility Enhancing Variables, by Factory

Mobility Enhancing Variables	Textile			Paper			Engine			Biscuit			Rubber		
	Sup.	Asp.	Non-Asp.	Sup.	Asp.	Non-Asp.	Sup.	Asp.	Non-Asp.	Sup.	Asp.	Non-Asp.	Sup.	Asp.	Non-Asp.
Present Factory															
Pct. skilled[c]	100.0[b]	72.5	55.9	100.0[b]	44.4	47.5	100.0[b]	86.5[a]	57.6	100.0[b]	50.0	40.2	100.0[b]	25.0	15.9
Pct. promoted in past	100.0[b]	6.3	9.5	100.0[b]	25.0	15.9	100.0[b]	61.8[a]	40.7	100.0[b]	20.0	17.6	100.0[b]	5.0	4.3
Mean seniority (years)	16.2[b]	10.8	10.6	24.4[b]	12.6	14.0	7.1[b]	5.8[a]	4.2	13.9[b]	9.0	9.0	5.3	3.7	3.7
Previous Experience															
Labor force seniority (yrs.)	21.5[b]	15.1	13.4	22.9[b]	14.3	15.7	12.3[b]	10.6[a]	7.5	17.1[b]	12.5	13.0	12.1	7.0	8.0
Pct. employed in other factory	69.0[b]	65.0[a]	44.1	18.4	11.1	31.1	72.7[b]	64.9[a]	31.8	25.0	25.0	42.6	38.5	25.0	23.2
Pct. experience in entry job	64.3[b]	52.5[a]	30.5	10.5	0.0	15.1	54.5[b]	40.5[a]	19.7	16.7	12.5	25.3	30.8	10.0	14.6
Pct. worked in another city	39.3	45.0	34.7	7.9	5.6	14.4	45.5[b]	24.3	12.1	33.3[b]	6.3	3.7	30.8	20.0	15.9
Non-Factory															
Mean age (yrs.)	40.6[b]	34.8	35.5	41.5[b]	29.8[a]	35.6	34.3[b]	29.1	27.5	43.7[b]	27.9[a]	31.4	32.9[b]	24.5[a]	31.6
Pct. educated[d]	38.1[b]	17.5	22.0	42.1[b]	50.0[a]	11.4	95.5[b]	81.1[a]	62.1	100.0[b]	87.5[a]	48.8	100.0[b]	80.0[a]	42.7
Pct. male	100.0	100.0	100.0	10.0[b]	94.4[a]	79.6	100.0	100.0	100.0	100.0[b]	100.0[a]	91.5	100.0[b]	100.0[a]	90.3
Pct. Brahman	17.6	2.5	2.5	10.5	0.0	9.6	40.9	32.4	30.3	83.3[b]	87.5[a]	42.6	53.8[b]	40.0[a]	20.7

[a] Significant difference at p < .05 between aspirers and non-aspirers. [b] Significant difference at p < .05 between supervisors and non-aspirers. [c] Worker at jobs for which the starting basic wage is more than Rs. 31 per month. [d] Finished more than four years of schooling.

job similar to the one for which they were brought into the mill. None of the other variables discriminated, neither experience within the present factory nor the non-factory attributes so important for the first three factories mentioned. In the Type C engine factory, all three sets of variables discriminate aspirers from non-aspirers. A significantly higher proportion of aspirers are already in the highest skilled jobs, have a past history of upward mobility, and have served longer with the company. The aspirers tend to have brought experience into the company; they have spent a longer time in the labor force, were twice as likely to have been employed in another factory, and to have performed a similar job in that factory. Among the non-factory variables the only attribute that discriminates is education, while the others which are not really functional to the factory—age per se and caste—do not discriminate.

These differences in the discriminating variables among the factories show rather strikingly the selective effect of the factory production process typology upon aspirations. But our general hypothesis calls for something more, that the worker sees in himself the same characteristics which distinguish the supervisors from most of the workers— that he measures himself against a realistic proto-supervisor type. Another look at Table LXXVII will indicate the evidence for this position. The superscript "b" indicates that the supervisors are significantly different from the non-aspirers on a given variable. A glance at the table will show that wherever an "a" appears, a "b" is found in the cell to the left. This shows that every variable which distinguishes the aspirers from the non-aspirers also distinguishes the supervisors from the non-aspirers. In the case of every variable except age, the sequence for the distinguishing variable is in the proper direction, that is, the aspirers fall between the supervisors and the non-aspirers. The function of age is interesting. In four of the five factories the aspirers are younger than both the supervisors and non-aspirers, indicating a decline in the general optimism of youth and the dropping out of the aspirer ranks of those who are still workers and have passed the average age when supervisors are appointed.

So far, we have discussed the differences between aspirers and non-aspirers within each factory but have said nothing about differences among factories in the proportions of workers who aspire to become supervisors. Table LXXVI showed that the percentage of supervisor aspirers ranged from 16.2 in the paper mill to 35.9 in the engine factory. What are the factors which produce a greater climate of optimism from one factory to another? Table LXXVIII shows the results of an attempt to see whether certain plausible variables would in fact predict the rankings of the companies in terms of their workers' aspiration levels.

TABLE LXXVIII

RANKING OF FACTORIES ON ASPIRATION LEVEL AND RELATED VARIABLES

Ranking Variables	Textile	Paper	Engine	Biscuit	Rubber
Per cent aspirers	2	5	1	4	3
Per cent promoted in past	4	3	1	2	5
Supervisor / P & M worker ratio	4	2	3	1	5
Per cent skilled	2	3	1	4	5
Mean current salary	2	3	1	4	5
Median job satisfaction score	5	4	3	1	2
Mean age (youngest)	5	4	2	3	1
Total no. of workers	1	3	2	5	4
Per cent of supervisors internally recruited	3	1	2	5	4

In the first row in the matrix the companies are ranked by the percentage of workers who aspire to become supervisor and the other rows show the rankings of the companies on other variables: percentage of workers who had moved from one skill rank to another within the company, the supervisor–P & M workers ratio, the percentage of skilled and semi-skilled workers, the mean current salary of all non-supervisory workers, median scores on a job satisfaction scale, the average age of all workers, the total number of workers, the percentage of supervisors who had been raised from the ranks rather than brought in from the outside. None of these variables gives a significant rank correlation with the ranking based upon the proportion of aspirers.

However, if we return to our earlier formulation, and visualize the laborer deciding that he will or will not become a supervisor on the basis of certain shared characteristics, then the apparent differences in aspiration level may just represent differences among the factories in the percentage of all workers who share the proto-supervisor characteristics in each factory. Using this hypothesis we would expect to find a constant proportion of the proto-supervisors in each factory aspiring to be supervisors.

Table LXXIX enables us to test this hypothesis. Age and seniority variables have been excluded because of their changing relationship to aspirations, and sex has been excluded because of the almost complete absence of female aspirers. Within the table, each cell represents for each factory the percentage of workers having the stated mobility-enhancing characteristics who aspired to be supervisors. The percentages followed by a superscript "a" are those which refer to the proto-supervisor attributes for each factory. An over-all glance at the table shows that a

191

TABLE LXXIX

PERCENTAGE OF P & M WORKERS POSSESSING MOBILITY-ENHANCING
ATTRIBUTES WHO ASPIRE TO BECOME SUPERVISORS

Mobility Variables	Textile	Paper	Engine	Biscuit	Rubber
Present Factory					
Skilled	30.5	14.0	45.7[a]	19.5	27.8
Promoted in past	18.2	18.8	48.8[a]	14.3	25.5
Earlier experience					
Employed in other factory	33.3[a]	6.4	53.3[a]	10.2	20.8
Worked in another city	30.6	5.9	52.9	9.1	14.3
Experienced in entry job	36.8[a]	0.0	53.6[a]	25.0	14.3
Non-Factory					
Educated	21.2	33.3[a]	49.6[a]	29.6[a]	31.4[a]
Brahmans	25.0	0.0	37.5	32.7[a]	32.0[a]
All supervisor aspirers	25.3	16.2	35.9	16.3	19.6

[a] Variables which distinguish between aspirers and non-aspirers.

minority of those with any mobility-enhancing characteristics are aspirers, the range going from zero to 53.6 per cent. However, if just the "a" percentages are examined, the cluster around one-third for all factories except the engine factory is very marked. The coefficient of variation for this distribution is only 6.7 per cent. The other variables, not marked, are much more dispersed. They have a coefficient of variation of 100.2 per cent. In other words, the percentages for the proto-supervisor variables are relatively uniform; the others vary both within the company and among companies. This is evidence for our earlier hypothesis that in the four companies the observed differences are the result of the relative frequency with which the proto-supervisor type is found among the laborers, rather than any general factor that produces a more optimistic atmosphere. Only in the engine factory, with its greater mobility, higher wages, use of present factory and earlier experience, and youthful labor force, does a generally higher aspiration level seem to be operating. Even here, the cluster of percentages around one-half is marked.

To summarize our findings on aspirations: most workers do not aspire to become supervisors, but a higher proportion of workers aspire than the supervisor-worker ratio would justify. The attributes which discriminate between supervisors and laborers vary from one factory to another. Three types of distinguishing variables are important: experience prior to present factory employment, experience in present company, non-factory social characteristics. Workers who aspire are distinguished from the non-aspirers by the same attributes which in their factory distinguish the supervisors from the workers. The proportion of workers who aspire in a factory is not a function of opportunities, but of the number of workers who share proto-supervisor attributes to become supervisors.

In the Type A factories, these are social characteristics. In the Type B textile mill previous experience is the key variable. And in the Type C engine factory education, previous experience, and current factory experience are all relevant. The Type C factory far exceeds all the others in both the wage and occupational category level of aspiration, followed in the latter by the Type B factory, then the Type A. In the level of relative wage aspirations, however, the new versus old factory dichotomy was most relevant.

Degree of Favorableness to the Company

This section has two interrelated aims, one substantive and the other methodological. Substantively, this part is concerned with the relationship between hierarchical rank among factory workers and the degree of favorableness in their attitudes toward the factory and its management, and with the differences in the level of favorableness among the factories. Methodologically, it is concerned with the problem of measuring attitudes using, in an Indian context, scaling devices developed in the West. In the course of the methodological argument, doubt will be cast upon the meaningfulness of the single question attitude measurement so common in Indian survey literature, but the problem of developing a more efficient device will be only partly resolved. The interrelationship between the methodological argument and the substantive findings is crucial since the correspondence between occupational rank and degree of favorableness is found to be equivocal at best. This lack of a consistent relationship is an important finding, but its validity depends upon the efficiency of the scales measuring both occupational rank and degree of favorableness. The absence of apparent relationship may be due to measurement errors in either variable, and this possibility makes it essential to refine these measures as much as possible. Hence the lengthy methodological considerations.

The Substantive Issue

For the moment, let us leave aside the question of interfactory differences in the degree of favorableness and turn our attention to the nature of the relationship between status and favorableness. One need not be a Marxian to hold the notion that satisfaction with an economic organization is directly correlated with the elevation of one's rank in it. Put more simply, each level will be less hostile or more favorable than the ones below it; this seems a natural corollary to any system of uneven distribution of rewards. There

194

is considerable evidence that this broad level generalization does in fact hold true in the industrialized countries of the West. For instance, Alex Inkeles, in a recent comparative analysis using data from the U.S.S.R., the United States, Germany, Italy, Sweden, and Norway, concluded:

"We have at hand fairly good data on job satisfaction in six countries covering a fair range of situations. There is a definite and unmistakable structure in the responses manifested from country to country. Those standing at the top are, as a rule, more satisfied than those in lower positions. Indeed, in every country the proportion who report job satisfaction decreases quite regularly as we descend the steps of the standard occupational hierarchy."[5]

In spite of this general theoretical presumption and the empirical evidence from Western countries, I entertained some doubt that the same pattern would emerge from Indian data. My suspicion, from an examination of the social organization of Indian society in general and Indian factories in particular, was that only the grossest differences in hierarchical occupational position would be systematically reflected in attitudes. In part, the differential satisfactions in the West rest upon the individual's notion of success as the achievement of high hierarchical position relative to other individuals in similar circumstances. The critical ingredient in this notion is achievement, which relies for its sustenance upon a fairly regular pathway of upward mobility and more than occasional movement of individuals up the occupational ladder. However, it will be recalled that there are few if any regular pathways, and the incidence of upward mobility is small indeed. Moreover, with the

[5] Alex Inkeles, "Industrial Man: The Relation of Status to Experience, Perception, and Value," *The American Journal of Sociology*, Vol. 66 (July 1960), p. 5.

linking (no matter how imperfect) of occupation to caste in the general society, the definition of success as "achieved occupational mobility" has scant support in the culture at large. And within the factories themselves, the overlay of seniority differentials, dearness allowance, proprietary rights in the job, and other features make the finer gradations in the hierarchical rankings of occupations of uncertain meaning either to the worker, his family, or indeed to the management itself. All of these considerations cast some doubt upon the extent to which favorableness to the company would march in step with occupational rank.

The Raw Data

At the end of the interview, each worker was asked to respond with a "yes," "no," or "can't say" for each of some twenty-five statements about his factory and its management, ranging from those that seemed extremely favorable through some neutral statements to those that seemed extremely unfavorable. They were, of course, not given in the order of their favorableness. The list of statements with the percentage of responses in each category is given in Table LXXX.

The Measurement of Favorableness. Most measurements of attitudes in Indian surveys confine themselves to simple dichotomies of yes and no on a single question with a residual undecided category. The attitude being surveyed is approached as directly as possible; for example, "Are you in favor of or opposed to birth control," or seed dibblers, or Russia, etc. The percentage of respondents on each side of the dichotomy is then taken to represent an approximation of a division of opinion in the group studied. In the more careful studies a standard error may be given to indicate the confidence limits for the projection from the

TABLE LXXX

Percentage Distribution of Responses to Statements About
Factory for All Workers

Statement	Yes	No	Can't Say
1. If the company's profits go down, the first thing they will do is fire the workers	48	36	16
2. I think I can be sure of my job as long as my work is good.	90	6	4
3. You have to work too long in this company to get a promotion.	73	20	7
4. Company officers think only of themselves.	66	25	9
5. In the long run this company will put it over on you.	74	17	9
6. While there is still a great deal to be done, the company is gradually improving its treatment of the workers.	67	28	5
7. The company exploits the workers every chance it gets.	68	26	6
8. The company shows favoritism in its promotion policy.	64	27	9
9. This company is good; however, it should pay a fair wage.	86	12	2
10. The workers in this factory are generally unhappy.	75	16	9
11. I work here only because I cannot find another job.	78	13	9
12. In the past few years, day by day things have become worse.	46	40	14
13. The work here is monotonous, it does not use all of my talents.	67	26	7
14. This company treats its workers better than most other companies.	52	27	21
15. If the company could, it would give all workers a wage increase.	61	31	8
16. This company looks after the workers' interests.	29	62	9
17. Sometimes this company is for the workers, sometimes it is not.	50	35	15
18. All companies are the same, this company is no better nor no worse than others.	71	12	17
19. On many occasions the company has put the interests of the workers above its own interests.	16	78	6
20. When the company promises you something you usually get it.	42	51	7

197

TABLE LXXX (continued)

Statement	Yes	No	Can't Say
21. A man can get ahead in this company if he tries.	47	45	8
22. The workers put as much over on the company as the company puts over on them.	52	36	12
23. If the company were more careful in its selection of supervisors the workers would be happier.	81	10	9
24. The workers in this factory are friendly and pleasant to work with.	88	10	2
25. If I could get an equally good job with any company I chose I would choose this one.	54	42	4
All statements	62	30	8

sample to the population. That this practice is not limited to Indian surveys but is characteristic of many polling operations can be seen from the fact that all of the studies used in Inkeles' analysis quoted above used some variant of a single question about whether the worker was satisfied or dissatisfied with his job. The response pattern indicated in Table LXXX illustrates how treacherous this procedure may be. The statements are about evenly divided between favorable and hostile statements. If we had selected almost any one of the favorable statements as our attitude measurer we would have concluded that the majority of the workers were favorably inclined toward the factory; if we had selected almost any one of the unfavorable statements, our conclusion would have been the opposite. Looking at the whole list, we see that in only three cases did the majority of the workers disagree with a statement, no matter whether it was positive or negative. It is evident that what is biasing the responses is what has been called "the acquiescence effect," that is, the tendency to agree to any generalization whatever.[6] Anxiety to please the interviewer is a sufficient explanation, but the respondents' motives for such a pattern need not detain us here. What is important is that the presence of this effect makes any absolute statement about the percentage of workers who really believed or disbelieved a given statement meaningless.

For our purposes, however, this is not a crippling handicap. If, instead of seeking to dichotomize the workers into favorable and unfavorable categories, we concern ourselves with the degree of favorableness and only seek to rank workers ordinally along this dimension with no attempt to set a zero point, then, if the acquiescence effect is spread among all workers, we can still rank individuals on their degree of favorableness to their factories by the number (suitably weighted) of positive and negative statements to which they subscribe. Because of the acquiescence effect, a worker's disagreement with a hostile statement will count as a more favorable response and thus be more heavily weighted than an agreement with a positive statement. This will not normally interfere with the validity of our measurement; it will only move all scores an undetermined but irrelevant number of points along the scale. Our rankings of degree, based upon a summation of response patterns, can remain valid even though we cannot say what percentage of the workers are generally favorable or unfavorable or even what percentage in reality agree or disagree with any given statement.

The scaling technique initially selected was drawn from the family of internal consistency scales, often called Likert scales after one of the pioneers in their development.[7] I do

6 See Bernard M. Bass, "Authoritarianism and Acquiescence," *Journal of Abnormal and Social Psychology*, 51:616-23 (Nov. 1955).
7 For a full elaboration of the rationale of this device, see the

not intend to go into the details of scale construction here, and I am sure that the procedure in Likert scaling is well known to many readers. However, there are several concrete points of procedure that the general reader must know, since the argument depends upon the effectiveness of the scale.

Once all the questionnaires had been filled in, the response patterns were scanned to screen out those statements that appeared most equivocal. First, those with too high a percentage of "can't say" responses were eliminated. Setting the limit at 10 per cent, statements 1, 12, 14, 17, 18 and 22 were rejected. Second, statements that are mutually contradictory and did not have complementary percentage distributions were discarded. There are three such pairs. It would seem logically impossible for 67 per cent of the workers to agree that "the company is gradually improving in its treatment of workers" (statement 6), and 60 per cent to agree that "things have gone from bad to worse" (statement 12). It would also seem unlikely that 88 per cent would truly agree that "all companies are the same, this one is no better or no worse than others" (statement 18), and 50 per cent agree that "this company treats its workers better than most others" (statement 14). Another unlikely pair is statement 11, "I work here only because I cannot find another job" (87 per cent agree), and statement 25, "If I could get an equally good job with any company I chose, I would choose this one" (54 per cent agree). The non-complementary percentages in these statements are further evidence of the acquiescence effect.

Next, the "discriminating power" of each statement was calculated. Put simply, this means that the respondents

---

classic by Gardner Murphy and Rensis Likert, *Public Opinion and the Individual*, New York: Harper, 1938.

were grouped into quartiles on the basis of the total number of favorable statements to which they agreed. Statements were then discarded if the percentage giving favorable and unfavorable responses did not differ significantly at the $p < .01$ level between the first and last quartile of respondents. Moreover, the percentages in the four quarters of the array had to descend or ascend in appropriate order. These four screening devices narrowed the acceptable statements down to 12 out of the original 25. It only remained to weight the statements according to their degree of favorableness toward the company. Each favorable response, a "yes" to a favorable statement or a "no" to an unfavorable statement, was weighted by a number from 7 to 4 and other responses from 4 to 1. The individual weights for favorable responses were roughly derived by calculating the percentage of favorable responses to a given statement as a ratio of the standard deviation of the percentage of favorable responses to all statements (turning the complement of each percentage into a standard score). The same procedure was followed separately for the unfavorable responses. The ratios were rounded off, and two points added to each to make all the weights positive. The basic logic of the weighting system is that the fewer people to subscribe to a given statement, the more extreme and thus the more favorable or unfavorable it will be. The following order of statements with their weights emerged.

The highest possible scale score is 68 if the worker gives the favorable response (yes or no) to every statement, and the lowest is 33 for all unfavorable responses, giving a range of 35 possible scale positions. In fact, only 23 positions were occupied. The frequency distribution of scale scores is given in Table LXXXII.

TABLE LXXXI

LIKERT SCALE WEIGHTS FOR DEGREE OF FAVORABLENESS

Statement	Yes	No	Can't Say
1. The workers in this factory are generally unhappy.	4	7	4
2. In the long run, this company will put it over on you.	4	7	4
3. Company officers think only of themselves.	3	6	3
4. The company exploits the workers every chance it gets.	3	6	3
5. The work here is monotonous, it does not use all my talents.	3	6	3
6. The company shows favoritism in its promotion policy.	3	6	3
7. This company looks after the workers' interests.	6	3	3
8. When the company promises you something, you usually get it.	6	3	3
9. A man can get ahead in this company if he tries.	5	3	3
10. If the company could, they would give all the workers a wage increase.	5	2	2
11. The workers in this factory are friendly and pleasant to work with.	4	1	1
12. This company is good; however, it should pay a fair wage.	4	1	1

TABLE LXXXII

SCALE SCORES FOR ALL WORKERS IN SAMPLE

Scale Score	No.	Scale Score	No.	Scale Score	No.
33	7	45	56	56	32
36	34	47	57	57	11
38	5	48	44	59	31
39	122	49	1	60	6
41	37	50	71	62	25
42	96	51	25	65	27
43	1	53	55	68	14
44	52	54	12	Total	821

Median = 46
Semi-Interquartile Range = 6

The relatively even spread of the frequencies across the scale is a reassuring indication that enough different levels of favorableness were measured to permit useful comparisons to be made of various worker categories, and we turn now to our substantive question: Are the hierarchical rankings of the workers reflected in differences in degree of favorableness?

Occupational Class and Likert Scale Score. Aside from the management, which was excluded from this study, there are three broad classes of workers in the factories reflected in the sample strata in Table LXXX. The term supervisor includes all those who directly control and oversee the work of others; those classified as clerks include cashiers, timekeepers, bookkeepers, etc.—all below the managerial level. All other workers are referred to as P & M workers. Since the scales are ordinal only, medians have been used to express the central tendency, and Table LXXXIII gives the median Likert scale scores for the combined factory workforce and for the five individual factories. The higher the score, the greater the degree of favorableness.

Table LXXXIII gives some rough support to the original

TABLE LXXXIII

MEDIAN LIKERT SCALE SCORES, BY FACTORY
AND BY OCCUPATIONAL CLASS

	Textile	Paper	Engine	Biscuit	Rubber	All Factories
P & M workers	42	44	45	50	46	45
Supervisors	44	47	53	52	48	47
Clerks	43	49	53	57	59	54
All workers	42	45	48	51	48	46

substantive generalization: degree of favorableness does seem to be associated with occupational class. The figures for the combined factory population, on the right, show the most favorable to the factory to be the clerks, followed by the supervisors. The differences among the medians are statistically significant, but not very striking.[8] Looking among the companies, the greater degree of favorableness of the clerks over the supervisors does not hold up for all five companies, but in all cases both groups have a higher median score than the P & M workers.

In all companies the supervisor-clerk versus P & M workers distinction is statistically significant, but the degree of distinction varies considerably. The supervisory and clerical groups come closest to the P & M workers in the textile mill, where the three groups are least clearly distinguished in the day-to-day operation of the plant. In this factory, the company employs semi-clerks who are stationed in the shop and not in a separate office, whose job it is to keep a running tally of production. As the name implies, they belong to both categories, clerks and P & M workers. Moreover, in this factory the supervisors are mainly jobbers, many of whom engage in some production activities in addition to their supervisory duties. Accordingly, the relatively small class differentiation in attitudes is not surprising.

The dispersion is roughly the same for all groups in all factories, the semi-interquartile range varying only one or two scale score points around a similar range of six for the combined factories. Along with this relatively constant

---

[8] The differences among the medians have been tested for heterogeneity by the medians test as described in Sidney Siegel, *Nonparametric Statistics for the Behavioral Sciences*, New York: McGraw-Hill Book Co., 1956, pp. 179-80.

dispersion within all groups and a fairly narrow differentiation among medians, the over-lap of scale scores among the three classes in all factories is very great. That is, there are many P & M workers with higher scale scores than some supervisors or clerks in all factories. In fact, in all factories scale scores over 60 and under 40 are shared by all three occupational classes. This implies, of course, that there are many more determinants of favorableness toward the factory than occupational class, but that occupational class does make a difference.

Gradations Within the Classes. While these relatively gross distinctions among occupational classes do roughly bear out Alex Inkeles' comparative findings on correlation between job satisfaction and hierarchical position,[9] although the confusion in the relative standing of clerks and supervisors needs further examination, it is relevant to ask whether more refined gradations within the three classes will also reflect a relationship between status and degree of favorableness.

In Table LXXXIV it can be noted that a significant relationship between the workers' current wages and their scale scores is found in either the supervisor or the clerical group in each factory, but not in any other group. In other words, of the two superior groups, in only one in each factory do the upper echelons favor the managerial attitudes toward the factory, and in none of the factories does the wage hierarchy among production and maintenance

---

[9] All the studies compared by Inkeles used some variant of a single question: "Are you satisfied or dissatisfied with your present job." His data, therefore, refer to job satisfaction proper. An examination of the statements used in the present scale indicates a much greater degree of heterogeneity, and thus the variable measured is called by the more general term favorableness. The logic of Inkeles' argument, however, would imply that both variables would behave alike under the influence of similar independent variables.

TABLE LXXXIV

CORRELATION BETWEEN CURRENT WAGE AND LIKERT SCALE
SCORE WITHIN EACH OCCUPATIONAL CLASS, BY FACTORY,
FOR PERMANENT WORKERS[a]

Occupational Class	Textile		Paper		Engine		Biscuit		Rubber	
	r	No.	r	No.	r	No.	r	No.	r	No.
Clerks	−.04	9	+.31[b]	5	+.35[b]	24	+.04	18	+.41[b]	23
Supervisors	+.46[b]	83	+.10	38	−.03	22	+.21[b]	12	+.06	12
P & M workers	−.01	127	−.04	93	−.05	87	+.08	78	−.05	90

[a] Temporary and *badli* workers have been omitted because of their variable monthly wage.
[b] Statistically significant at the $p < .01$ level.

workers correspond even roughly with the degree of favorableness. While these low correlations within the occupational classes do not dismiss the differences among classes shown in Table LXXXIII, they do imply that for most workers in the factory only the grossest differentiations in hierarchical position tend to produce different degrees of favorableness.

Refinements of Measurement. Since this partial contravention of the findings of studies in industrialized countries concerning occupational status and job satisfaction rests upon the absence of relationship in the data at hand, it is a clear possibility that the apparent absence may result from the crudeness of our measurement of the variables rather than from a genuine lack of relationship. We can never dismiss this possibility entirely, and it is an especially strong possibility when we are dealing with such cumbersome devices as attitude scales, but we can attempt to redefine and remeasure our variables to see if a relationship will then emerge.

Turning first to the use of wages to measure hierarchical position, while the current wage does reflect a worker's relative reward for his labor, it reflects very imperfectly his position within the *occupational* hierarchy, especially among the P & M workers. As we pointed out earlier, the current take-home wage includes dearness allowance which, since it is regressive as a percentage of total wage, tends to narrow differences among the skill levels. Moreover, annual increments and the short term exigencies of the supply of certain scarce skills at a given point of time tend to obscure further the wage hierarchy. The skill grades, however, would seem to approach more closely the concept of the relative status of occupations with which the Western studies have been concerned. Table LXXXV gives the median Likert scale scores for the five skill grades among the P & M workers in each factory. It will be recalled that Skill Grade I, the highest, is not represented in two of the factories.

Looking down the median columns for each factory in Table LXXXV, we see quickly that there is no general relationship between skill grade and degree of favorableness among the P & M workers, as measured by the Likert

TABLE LXXXV

MEDIAN LIKERT SCALE SCORE BY SKILL GRADE
AMONG P & M WORKERS, BY FACTORY

Skill Grade	Textile		Paper		Engine		Biscuit		Rubber		All Factories	
	Med.	No.	Med.	No.	Med.	No.	Med.	No.	Med.	No.	Med.	No.
I	—	—	41	8	45	10	—	—	62	3	46	21
II	42	4	45	3	50	6	45	6	42	4	45	22
III	41	74	42	10	43	33	50	5	46	4	42	127
IV	41	17	45	36	44	21	50	30	50	7	46	111
V	42	63	42	54	50	33	51	57	48	84	46	291
All P & M workers	42	158	44	111	50	103	50	98	47	102	45	572

Scale. Having refined the measure of hierarchical status without enhancing the apparent relationship between status and favorableness, we need now to refine our measure of the dependent variable, the degree of favorableness.

It will be recalled that in our earlier discussion of the acquiescence effect we argued that while it would obscure the "true" distribution of workers into a favorable versus unfavorable classification, it would not normally interfere with the validity of the scale, just move all scores a constant number of points along the continuum. The one danger in this conclusion is that the pattern of acquiescence may be different for unfavorable as compared to favorable statements. This might make different combinations of varyingly weighted positive and negative responses unequal even though they might give the same scale score. It is difficult to know this from the pattern of responses without somehow measuring the "true" degrees of intensity represented by each positive and negative statement.

It was decided to guard against this possibility by limiting the scale to positive statements only, so that each worker would be rated according to his performance on a single type of response. It was also decided to employ a more rigorous scaling device, one that would have some internal evidence of validity and of the unidimensionality of the variable being measured—degree of favorableness. The scale type best fitting these qualifications is the scalogram, often called the Guttman Scale after its originator.[10] It will be recalled that in Guttman scales the

[10] For the original and still classic discussion of this scale type see S. A. Stouffer, et al., *The American Soldier: Measurement and Prediction*, Princeton University Press, 1950.

statements are ranked in order of number of favorable responses and the individuals ranked in order of number of statements to which the respondent agreed (in our example using only positive statements). A random sample of 100 workers was drawn from the full 821 and the following statements from among the favorable ones fitted the scalogram pattern. They are listed in degree of favorableness.

The workers put as much over on the company as the company puts over on them.

On many occasions, the company has put the interest of the workers above its own interests.

This company looks after the workers' interests.

A man can get ahead in this company if he tries.

If I could get an equally good job with any company I chose, I would choose this one.

If the company could, they would give all workers a wage increase.

While there is still a great deal that can be done, the company is gradually improving in its treatment of its workers.

This company is a good company; however, it should pay a fair wage.

That is to say, if a worker agreed to the first statement, he also agreed to all statements below it, or, more generally, if he agreed to any statement in the scale, he also agreed to all those below it and none above it. This scale pattern was violated in a little less than 10 per cent of the responses, making it an inelegant but acceptable measure. It was also tested for reliability and yielded a coefficient of reliability of $r_{tt} = .75$, showing that the scale discriminates among individuals fairly well.[11] The standard error is only 1.11 scale units. It will be noted that the surviving statements are more limited in their scope than the full set of 25 statements. They are mostly concerned with management's intentions and actions toward the workers.

The above set of scaled statements, then, give nine possible scale types ranging from a response pattern in which a worker agreed with all eight statements, making him the most favorable to the company, to a pattern in which he agreed with none. This new scale correlates reasonably well (r = .56), but not completely with the Likert Scale.

Having refined both our measure of occupational status and degree of favorableness, we can again return to our substantive question. It will be recalled that we showed a mild relationship between membership in the broad occupational classes of supervisor, clerk, and P & M worker. The Likert scale did not reveal any clear relationship between rank and degree of favorableness within the P & M class where the bulk of the workers are found. Does the Guttman Scale show any such relationship? Table LXXXVI shows the percentage in each scale type for each job class. It will be recalled that the higher the scale score the greater the degree of favorableness, but the occupational grades are numbered with the highest at 1 and the lowest at 5.

Table LXXXVI indicates that there is a statistically significant relationship between occupational grade and degree of favorableness, but an examination of the percentages in the table shows little regularity. All grades

[11] The test used is given in C. J. Hoyt, "Test Reliability Estimated by Analysis of Variance," *Psychometrika*, 6:153-160 (1941).

TABLE LXXXVI

PERCENTAGE IN EACH SCALE TYPE BY OCCUPATIONAL GRADE
FOR ALL WORKERS IN ALL FACTORIES

Occupa-tional Grade	Degree of Favorableness									Number in Sample
	0	1	2	3	4	5	6	7	8	
I	—	4.8	19.0	9.5	47.6	14.3	9.5	4.8	—	21
II	—	—	27.3	4.5	9.1	9.1	18.2	4.5	27.3	22
III	3.1	2.4	16.5	16.5	26.8	5.5	18.9	7.9	2.4	127
IV	0.9	5.4	15.3	17.1	13.5	11.7	11.7	9.0	15.3	111
V	1.0	6.2	6.2	22.7	9.6	6.5	12.0	21.6	14.1	291
All grades	1.4	4.9	11.5	19.1	15.6	7.3	13.6	14.9	11.7	572

$X^2 = 76.8$, df = 21, p $<$ .01
Gamma[12] = —.14

have a median score of either 4 or 5, and there is no progression from highest grade to lowest. Moreover, gamma, which measures the degree and direction of association, shows only a mild over-all relationship (—.14), and then in the opposite direction to that which our theory predicted. In other words, there is a slight, statistically significant tendency for the lower occupational groups to be more favorable. The association is so slight, however, and X^2 is so notoriously responsive to the size of N, that I would be inclined to attribute this relationship to test "noise," that is, inaccuracies of measurement. In any event, the evidence does not support our notion of a positive association between hierarchical ranking and degree of favorableness.

Status and Favorableness Summary. The above analysis leads us to conclude that in the Indian factories studied

[12] Cf. L. A. Goodman and W. H. Kruskal, "Measurement of Association for Cross-Classification," *Journal of American Statistical Association*, 49: 732-64 (1954).

there is a genuine but mild positive relationship between membership in the broad occupational classes and degree of favorableness toward the factory and its management. No relationship appeared below the level of supervisory and clerical workers when rank is measured either by current wages or occupational grade and when favorableness is measured by either a Likert or Guttman scale.

As was pointed out at the outset, however, it is impossible to demonstrate conclusively the absence of a relationship, since the apparent absence may be due to the inaccuracy of our measuring devices. I feel sure that there is in the reader's mind some doubt about the effectiveness of any such attitude measures for Indian factory workers. When the matter is pressed, the doubt seems to arise from the presumed ignorance and illiteracy of the workers. To allay this anxiety, literate workers' scores were compared with non-literate workers' scores and no significant differences emerged in any factory. Nor did test scores correlate with the amount of education the worker received. The relatively small percentage of "can't say" responses is not conclusive evidence of lack of ambiguity, but, on the other hand, it does not support the notion of indecisiveness on the part of the worker. It should also be noted that the stereotype of the illiterate, uneducated worker is certainly not a true picture of most of the workers in this study. Some 73.1 per cent of all the workers were literate by actual test, while 69.1 per cent had attended grammar school or higher. It is still possible that there are some other psychological attributes peculiar to Indian workers that make such attitude measurements unreliable. This problem is certainly worthy of study, since the attitude measuring devices are now largely parochial, that is, they have been tested and standardized only for Western audiences. In the meantime, however, I would maintain that they are at least superior to the single-question attitude measurements now in such common use.

Finally, it should be pointed out that the relationship between occupational rank and job satisfaction described in Inkeles' comparative survey might not hold up for such fine gradations as we have used here. The occupational classes he was dealing with were roughly equivalent to our broadest classes, where the relationship also emerged in our data. Perhaps it is asking too much to have the degree of favorableness follow the more refined ranking of wage differences or skill rankings within a broad occupational class.

Differences Among Factories. If we leave aside for the moment the methodological question of the validity of the scales, what do the differences among factories reflect? Looking at the average scores by factory for both the Likert and Guttman scales given in the bottom rows of Tables LXXXIII and LXXXV, we can conclude that differences among the factories in the average degree of favorableness do not correspond with differences in average current wage level among P & M workers any more than intra-factory differences reflected this variable. In view of our general theme, however, we might expect such differences to coincide with our production process typology. We might entertain various hypotheses concerning the average degree of favorableness that the workers in Type A, B, or C should have. For instance, we might expect favorableness to decline as the departure from the traditional social organization increased. In that case we should expect favorableness to be highest in the paper, biscuit and rubber factories, next highest in the textile mill, and lowest in the engine factory. Or one might

213

suppose that since all of the factories represent a departure from traditional social organization and that the factory is an alternative form of organization with its own internal logic, that the factory most closely approximating the ideal type would have the greatest degree of favorableness, just as it had the highest aspiration levels. If this were so, the order of favorableness should descend from C to A. An examination of Tables LXXXIII and LXXXV indicates that neither of these alternative hypotheses is confirmed.

In both tables the division of new versus old factories seems to indicate degree of favorableness, although the variation among factories is not very great. It is difficult to know precisely what this means. One might suspect that as in earlier discussions this meant the determining factors were the social characteristics of the workers. However, separate tests of the relevance of each social characteristic to degree of favorableness in each company did not show any significant relationships. In particular, age and seniority, which parallel the new versus old factory, do not correlate with degree of favorableness. It may be a preference for the direct managerial participation of the owning family, or perhaps the clearly superior physical plants of the newer factories. Our data give no clue to the source of the correspondence between age of the factory and degree of favorableness.

SUMMARY AND THEORETICAL IMPLICATIONS

To tie together the many sections of our discussion of the functions of the individual worker and the hierarchy, let us link it with our general thesis on the nature of the transformation which the factory is presumed to make in the traditional social organization. The data presented in this chapter, together with some of the earlier data, permit us to hazard an opinion as to whether these five factories in general or some among them reflect in their social organization the nub of the transformation envisaged in the Introduction: a shift from ascribed to achieved status as a basis of hierarchical rankings, the rising of aspiration levels, and the tying of aspirations to performance. To start with status, the factory with its emphasis upon task performance and opportunities for upward mobility is presumed to be the antithesis of the static, ascribed status society which surrounds it, or at least it is supposed to differ significantly in degree. The term "quality" should have a very different meaning for the factory and for the society at large. It is therefore of considerable interest to look back at our data to determine the extent to which the factory hierarchy parallels the "quality" hierarchy in the outside society. The two keys to status in the non-factory society are caste and ethnic affiliation and education (such a large proportion of the population is literate that it is not a good status discriminator); status within the factory is measured by occupational category and current wage. In general, the full hierarchy of caste is reflected very poorly in the factory rankings. It was true, however, that the ends of the continuum, that is, whether or not one is a Brahman or a member of the Backward Classes, made a difference. Clerks were largely Brahmans, as were either the majority or the upper echelons of the supervisory personnel. Among the P & M workers, however, being a Brahman was no help. Belonging to the Backward Classes was a hindrance at all levels. In their middle ranges, caste or ethnic affiliation seemed to make little difference. Educational differences operate in much the same way as caste rankings. Extreme differences in educational attainment

215

are important but minor gradations are not; education sorts out the workers into supervisor, clerical, and P & M classes, but, except for some supervisory levels, has little effect on gradations within these classes.

While both caste and education are measures of "quality" in the external society, caste is a measure of ascribed status par excellence, and education an achieved status attribute. Our thesis concerning the substitution of achieved for ascribed status requires that caste give way to education as a basis for ranking. In fact, however, the two are so intertwined that it is difficult to separate them, and one supports the other. To the extent that we can separate them in this study by holding one constant and determining whether the other one is still reflected in variations in position within the factory, the basic classifying variable seems to be education, supporting the notion of the growing supremacy of achieved status attributes. In one sense, however, this conclusion is misleading. While education is truly an achieved status attribute in the general society, it is not achieved in the factory. That is to say, the factory theoretically should reward on the basis of job performance, and gradations in education must contribute to superior job performance in order to qualify fully as attributing to achieved status in the factory itself. Certainly the simplicity of tasks in most of the factories cannot utilize any but the most minimal education, and we must therefore consider the prizing of education as relating more to "quality" as defined by the general society than to "quality" as required by the production processes. This is especially so when we recall that the newer the factory the more its recruitment practices reach out for more workers with more education, regardless of the demands of the work to be performed.

Unfortunately we have no measure of job performance against which we could lay the workers' rankings in the factory. We would need this to determine whether achieved status based upon skill and industry are truly discriminating variables. We do have collateral evidence, however, that any such matching is very crude indeed. In the first place, most of the companies themselves have no measure of the individual worker's performance. In most factories productivity becomes relevant only when a vacancy occurs at a higher level, and here the workers report that while they think job performance should be the basis of promotion, "influence" is, in fact, the prime determinant. Moreover, vacancies at skilled levels were uncommon, often were filled by workers recruited externally, and most workers stayed at exactly the same level throughout their entire career in the factory. The hierarchical rankings within the factory are themselves somewhat confused. It is very rare that individual performance is reflected in wage differentials. The textile factory operated on a piece-rate system for most of its semi-skilled workers, the weavers and spinners particularly, but this system is subject to the same limitations as a job performance incentive system. An individual's performance depends upon the looms or spindles assigned to him, the efficiency of the servicing of the machinery, the amount of work available, and the classic anxieties and sanctions against rate-busting that are enforced by fellow workers. The bonus incentive system used in the engine factory, combining individual and group performance, seems to be more satisfactory. For the worker not under one of these piece-rate or bonus systems, increased performance brings no reward at all, so he is motivated to produce the necessary minimum to retain his property rights in the job, but

217

little more. The loitering around the compound of Indian factory workers is notorious, and the retaliation of the company with long working hours is equally notorious.

Moreover, the wage differentials themselves are very unclear reflectors of management's evaluation of the workers' worth. We have shown that the dearness allowance and the annual increment systems thoroughly obscure what the companies conceive to be a skill-based wage slab system. We have also noted that, in some companies at least, dearness allowance fluctuations are more important to the total wage of a worker than piece-rate performance or an increase in the basic wage as a new skill level is reached. And, aside from dearness allowance increases, the workers' main hope for a wage increase is that there would be an across-the-board raise coming out of the next union-management negotiations. In addition, there is the annual lottery of the bonus which, in the workers' eyes, depends upon fate, the union's strength, and the company's magnanimity, in about that order, and certainly not upon their own efforts. To a considerable extent, the effect of the factory in introducing achieved status attributes as a ranking basis and linking aspirations to productivity depends upon developing a more rational system whereby wage differentials are tied more closely to performance. The trend is not in this direction.

We turn now from the general question of the role of achieved status in "the factory" to inter-factory comparisons. The three factories types differed radically in the extent to which achieved status provided the basis for gradations within the factory. In the Type A factories, the primary group orientation of the production process made it natural that the supervisory function be in the hands of socially superior individuals rather than those whose superiority derived from experience and achievement in this or other factories. Here age, caste, and education (as pointed out above, ascribed status insofar as the factory is concerned) were the primary considerations. There is nothing in the worker's performance in the factory that can influence these attributes, and thus they most certainly can not be used as work incentives. Our data indicate that the workers in Type A factories are well aware of the nature of the qualifications for supervisors and judge their chances of becoming supervisors on whether they possess those "quality" attributes which make them potential supervisor candidates.

In the Type B factory, linked as it is to a large industry, the major supervisor-defining attributes are related to work experience prior to reaching the present factory. While this is technically achieved status, like education it is something the worker brings to his present factory and cannot be achieved in it. If we ignore the boundaries of a particular factory, Type B factories can provide upward mobility based upon achieved status largely by inter-unit mobility, but within a single factory it is ascribed attributes that count. Performance within the factory is not geared to upward mobility chances, and the workers are well aware of this in judging their supervisory candidacy upon the basis of their past experience alone.

In the Type C factory, achieved status is relevant to supervisory appointment. We have no measure of job performance per se, but seniority, skill, and past record of upward mobility within the present factory, as well as experience in other factory employment, all mark off the supervisors and those who hope to become supervisors. Among the "social quality" attributes, only education was also a proto-supervisory trait. It seems clear that only in the Type C factory has achieved status based upon work performance in the present factory genuinely emerged as a criterion for upward mobility.

Aside from supervisory promotions, the bases of the rankings among P & M workers in all the factories are none too clear. While the sets of attributes discussed above do serve to distinguish supervisors and those who aspire to become supervisors—except for age and seniority, which are tied in with the annual increment system of basic wages—none of the ascribed or achieved attributes studied serve to distinguish the different ranks or wage levels among the P & M workers. One can only conclude that the P & M skill grade membership depends upon some set of attributes not covered in this study, or that such promotions and appointments are a most haphazard process based upon ad hoc decisions that as yet fall into no distinctive pattern. This, of course, further reduces the effectiveness of potential upward mobility as a motivator of higher productivity and weakens the impact of the factory in effecting a substitution of achieved for ascribed status in the general society.

But then our data showed that the actual upward mobility in most of the factory types has been relatively rare in the past—status immobility has not surrendered to rapid vertical and horizontal mobility. There is even some question whether in most factories the amount of upward mobility is more than an individual's fortune might provide him in the general society. The notion that India's has been a society of status immobility, reinforced by simplistic notions about caste and the fixity of inherited occupations, has no doubt underestimated the amount of fluctuation over time in family fortunes, particularly among urban families. What little mobility does occur in the factories can easily fit into the flexible framework of the traditional ascribed status system. Differences in the amount of internal mobility among the various factory types are, however, genuine. The slab-like structures with very few workers at the skilled levels, very low turnover, and external recruitment of artisans, keep the mobility rate very low in the Type A factories. In the Type B textile mill the range of skills is great enough to make a substantial amount of upward mobility possible, but the tendency to recruit workers who have acquired their skills elsewhere keeps the internal mobility to a minimum. Mobility is highest in the Type C engine factory for it has the necessary elaboration of skill structure, limitations upon the external recruitment of skills, and a procedure for "training-up" men in advanced skills without having to move them from one occupational title to another. In this factory almost half the workers had experienced some job mobility; in none of the others had even one-fourth of the workers been mobile at all.

It is difficult to make any statements at all about the relative aspiration levels of factory workers and non-factory workers because of the complete lack of information on the latter. We have, of course, the general characterization of Indians in general as fatalistic, but it is impossible to relate this to any individual's, particularly any urban dweller's, estimate of his own life chances. As has been pointed out, the factory workers have already done fairly well by securing property rights in a job that at its worst pays more than do the sources of income of half of the earners in the city. Our data do show that in all the factories more workers expect to be promoted than the frequency of promotions in the past would seem to justify, so that in one sense aspiration levels are unrealistically high. On the other hand, the workers are realistic in that they seem to be aware of the set of attributes which distinguish supervisors from workers in their particular factories and judge their own promotional possibilities in these terms. Those who aspire are distinguished from the non-aspirers by the same sets of attributes in any given factory as the supervisors are so differentiated. This means, of course, that the use of aspirations as a motivation to higher productivity is effective only when the proto-supervisory attributes are in fact related to performance within the factory, to internally achieved status attributes. As we have seen, only in the Type C factory is this so. It is interesting to note that it is in this factory that aspirations are highest, both absolutely in terms of the percentage of aspirers—more than a third—and in terms of the number of the proto-supervisor types who aspire—about half. In the other factories, from 15 to 25 per cent of all laborers, and about a third of the proto-supervisors, aspire to become supervisors. In no case is it likely that all who aspire will succeed.

THE FUTURE

To summarize our conclusions, then, concerning the possible effect of the factory in producing the general transformation outlined in the Introduction—substituting contract for status, decreasing the primary group organization of work, encouraging the growth of achieved status attributes, increasing mobility, and raising aspiration levels—the internal organization of the factories does not represent nearly so sharp a break with the past as might be expected. Among the factories, only Type C—the engine factory—seems to embody all these attributes in substantial amounts. To a considerable extent it is this that is

222

meant when the engine factory and its owners are called and consider themselves to be modern and progressive, and most estimates of the impact of the factory on the non-industrialized society have in mind a social organization which will eventually reach Type C form. The other forms are thought of as imperfect, interim stages, as temporary compromises with the indigenous culture, to give way under careful nurture and the inevitable logic of superior, rational economic production standards. While the inevitability of the movement toward Type C establishments may be true for the long run, current short-run tendencies are not in this direction. Pressures upon management from both unions and government are toward more and more minute job specification, guaranteeing a job title to a worker and a wage based upon the kind of work he does, not how well he does it. The Type C factory was, even at the time of the study, under great pressure to create the pigeonhole structure of Type B, and as the plant ceases to expand or a surplus labor force with the requisite skills becomes locally available as it is for the Type B textile mill, the engine factory may lose its "modern" character. Once the pigeonholes become set in a collective bargaining agreement, every change will be subject to full-scale negotiations and become part of the bargaining package. The least flexible form of organization becomes perpetuated by the tendency of the unions to fight for, and arbitrators to award, across-the-board increases in wages, rather than systems of merit increases where the decisions about relative merit lie with management. The boundaries of occupational titles tend to become fixed, self-perpetuating, and resistant to crossing. Schemes for the decasualization of labor, including such devices as that prevalent in Bombay where preferential hiring is given to textile workers registered on government rolls by occupational title, will move matters even further toward the Type B pattern. Even the Type A factories, now probably the most numerous throughout India, are tending toward more and more minute and fixed pigeonhole categories. The submissions of management and union to the labor tribunal for a proposed labor contract at the time of the study had moved conditions a considerable distance in this direction. It is a moot question whether the primary group form of organization of production can survive the pressures for the pigeonhole structure. And spreading over all the forms of organization, the marginal role of basic wage differentials, the increasing lack of fit between received wage differentials and status hierarchies based upon skill or any other performance criteria, makes it difficult to lead India's industrial labor market to any sort of rationalization. Above all, the combination of these factors makes it very difficult to build into the factory system any set of individual motivations which will enhance the worker's commitment to the goals of the company and increase individual productivity.

In short, if the introduction of the factory is to be the sole or even the major catalyst in the modernization of Indian society in terms of the transformation from *Gemeinschaft* to *Gesellschaft*, the evidence of the present study indicates that modernization may be a long way off.

APPENDIX A

QUESTIONNAIRE

1. Complete name ....
2. Name of factory or mill ....
3. Job in factory ....
4. Address ....
5. Date of birth or age .... 6. Male or Female ....
7. Highest grade completed in school
   and year when completed ....
8. Religion .... Caste .... Sub-Caste ....
9. Ever married .... Never married .... If married, when? ....
   Does your wife live here? .... Yes .... No .... Widowed ......
   Divorced .... If divorced, remarried? .... Yes .... No ....
10. Mother Tongue .... Marathi .... Gujarati ....
    Telegu .... Kanadi .... Hindi ....
11. What other languages do you speak? ....
    Marathi .... Gujarati .... Hindi ....
    Telegu .... Kanadi .... English ....
12. Literacy

Language	Marathi	Gujarati	Hindi	Telegu	Kanadi	English
Highest						
Middle						
A Little						
Cannot Read						

13. (a) Have you lived in Poona all of your life? Yes .... No ....
    If No, when did you come to Poona? ....
    From where? ....
    (b) If Yes, how many years has your family lived in Poona?
    .... Where did your family come from? ....
    (c) What was (is) your father's occupation? ....
    What was (is) your grandfather's occupation? ....
14. What other members of your family live with you? ....

Earners

	Relation	Age	Occupation or Job	Monthly Income	How long Resided
1.					
2.					
3.					
4.					
5.					

Non-Earners

	Relation	Age	Educand?	Looking For Work?	How Long Resided
1.					
2.					
3.					
4.					
5.					

15. When were you first employed by your present company? Month .... Year ....

16. In your factory/mill what is the distinction between Permanent and Temporary workers?
    1. ....
    2. ....
    3. ....
    4. ....
    5. ....

17. Are you a Temporary .... Substitute .... Permanent .... Worker?

The Following Questions Are For Permanent Workers Only

18. How long after you were hired did you become Permanent?
    ....

19. Have you worked continuously since you were first employed by this firm? Yes .... No ....
    If No, when were you Unemployed and why?

Dates

	Began	Ended	Reason
1.			
2.			
3.			
4.			
5.			
6.			
7.			
8.			

20. Starting from the beginning, what different jobs have you done in this company? ....
    Give the dates during which you held each job and the monthly wage.

226

	Job	Dept.	Beginning	End	Total Monthly Pay
1.					
2.					
3.					
4.					
5.					
6.					
7.					
8.					
9.					
10.					

21. What were the reasons for the job change?

1.	Took the place of someone who left	
2.	The company expanded	
3.	Reorganization of personnel	
4.	Requested a transfer	
5.	Someone was on leave	
6.	Other	
7.		
8.		

22. Other than those mentioned, are there any jobs you do temporarily during somebody's absence or when the company needs extra men?   Yes .... No ....

How many days did you work at each during past year?

	Job	Dept.	No. of Days	Total Monthly Pay	Reason
1.					
2.					
3.					
4.					
5.					
6.					
7.					
8.					

23. Do any of them pay a higher wage than your present wage? Yes .... No ....

24. What was your total monthly wage when you were first hired? ....

25. What is your total monthly wage now? ....

26. Give the wage increases and the reasons for them that you have had with this company.

	New Monthly Wage	Date	Reason		Reason
1.				1.	Industrial court ruling
2.				2.	Annual increment
3.				3.	Moved to a higher job
4.				4.	Dearness allowance increased
5.				5.	Others
6.				6.	
7.				7.	
8.				8.	
9.				9.	
10.				10.	

The Following Questions Are For Temporary and Substitute Workers

27. Do you want to be a permanent worker in this factory?
Yes .... No ....
28. Do you expect to become a permanent worker?
Yes .... No ....
29. If yes, how much longer will it take? ....
30. Are you now assigned to a specific job? Yes .... No ....
Explain ....
31. On the average, about how many days per month have you worked during the last year?
What is the most days? ....
What is the least days? ....
32. What sort of work do you do on the days you do not work at this factory? ....
33. Start from the beginning, what different jobs have you held in this firm? For Temporary give the length of time per job. For Substitute give the average number of days per month.

	Job	Dept.	Temporary or Substitute	No. of Days	Daily Wage
1.					
2.					
3.					
4.					
5.					
6.					

34. Is there any favoritism in the assignment of jobs?
Yes .... No ....
If so, how does it work? ....
35. What has been your monthly income for each of the past six months?

1956

December	November	October	September	August	July

The Following Questions Are For All Workers

36. Before you were employed by this firm what other jobs did you have?

	Place	Factory	Job and Dept.	Temporary, Substitute or Permanent	Monthly Wage	Dates	Reason for Leaving
1.							
2.							
3.							
4.							
5.							

37. When you first started looking for a job, how long did it take?
....

38. After you were first employed, were you ever unemployed?
Yes .... No ....
If yes, when, for how long and why? ....

	Dates	Job	Dept.	Reasons
1.				
2.				
3.				
4.				
5.				

39. From what you have told me let me try to reconstruct your work history.

Year	Job Status	Pay	Year	Job Status	Pay

40. How did you get this job? ....
41. [Following questions to be asked if answers are not given to question above; be sure all are answered]
    (a) Did you send in a written application? Yes .... No ....
        If yes, did it help? Yes .... No ....
    (b) Did you answer an advertisement in the newspaper?
        Yes .... No ....
    (c) Did the union help in finding a job? Yes .... No ....
        If yes, what kind of help? ....
    (d) Before you got this job, did you know anybody who worked here? Yes .... No .... If yes, what job did he do here? ....
        How were you acquainted? ....
        Did they help in getting this job? Yes .... No ....
        If yes, how? ....
    (e) Have you ever been registered with the employment exchange? Never .... Previously, but not now ....
        Now ....
        Did they ever help you in getting a job? Yes .... No ....
        If yes, when and what kind? ....
        If no, do you know anyone personally who got a job through the exchange? Yes .... No ....
        If yes, when and how? ....
42. How important do you think influence is in getting a good job?
    1. The most important thing ....
    2. Important but other things are more important ....
    3. It counts a little but not much ....
    4. Not at all important ....
43. If you had some available money could you get a better job?
    Yes .... No ....
    If yes, how much would it cost, and what kind of job?

	Job	Money			Job	Money
1.			3.			
2.			4.			

44. If you lost your job tomorrow would you try to get another factory job? Yes .... No ....
    If no, what would you do? ....
    If yes, what factories would you try and for what job?

	Factory-Mill	Place
1.		
2.		
3.		
4.		
5.		

How would you go about trying for them? ....
What would you do? ....
What do you think your chances would be? ....
How long would you be out of work? ....

45. Have you applied elsewhere for a job? Yes .... No ....
If yes, where? ....
When did you first apply? ....

46. When you were unemployed, what did you live on? ....
How much did your relatives help? ....
Others ....

47. Each time, how many jobs did you apply for before you got one?
....
Have you thought of going elsewhere? Yes .... No ....
Why didn't you? ....

48. Do you have any other source of income? Yes .... No...........
If yes, what other source? ....
How much does it bring (monthly if possible)? ....

49. How does your family feel about your job? Good ....
Fair .... Bad ....
Do they like your job? Yes .... No ....
Do they think you could do better elsewhere?
Yes .... No ....

50. (a) In your factory what are the best jobs?

	Job	Department	Pay
1.			
2.			
3.			
4.			

(b) Do you think you can get them? Yes .... No ....
(c) What are the worst jobs in the factory? ....

51. What is the highest job you think you can get in this factory?
....
How long do you think it would take you? ....

52. In getting promoted, what should count most?

1.	Seniority	
2.	Good job performance	

53. If you belonged to another caste do you think you would have
a better chance for advancement? Yes .... No ....
If yes, which caste? ....
Brahman .... Maratha .... Harijan .... Gujarati ....
Kanadi .... Hindi-speaker .... Christian ....

54. If you could get a job outside of this factory what jobs would
you like to have?

	Job	Dept.			Job	Dept.
1.			4.			
2.			5.			
3.			6.			

Do you know anyone who holds these jobs? ....

55. If you had a choice of the following three types of jobs which would you take?

1.	Guaranteed permanent job	
2.	Higher pay	
3.	Chance for advancement	

56. If you could have afforded an education how much would you have wanted? .... For what?......................

57. (a) How much and what kind of an education would you like a son of yours to have? ....

    (b) How much would it cost? ....

    (c) If your son's luck were good, what would be the best job he could get? ....

    (d) How much do you think it would pay? ....

    (e) If your luck were good what is the highest job you could get? ....

    (f) How much do you think it would pay? ....

58. (a) Are you a member of a union? Yes .... No ....
    If yes, what union ....? When did you join? ....

    (b) If no, why did you not join? ....

    (c) What should a union do for its members? ....

59. When you have accumulated enough money do you expect to quit the factory and go back to the village? Yes .... No ....
If yes, how long will it take? ....

APPENDIX B

Caste	Textile	Paper	Engine	Biscuit	Rubber	Total Factory	Poona Population
Brahmans							
Konkanastha	28	—	41	23	29	121	385
Others	70	65	184	67	131	517	716
Total number	98	65	225	90	160	638	1101
Per Cent	4.2	10.8	36.7	56.3	30.2	15.0	19.7
Marathas							
Marathas	1034	176	127	38	104	1479	1219
Kunbi	14	—	—	—	—	14	16
Total Number	1048	176	127	38	104	1493	1235
Per Cent	44.8	29.2	20.7	23.6	19.6	35.2	22.1
Intermediate							
CKP	1	—	—		5	6	63
Mali	99	38	22	5	19	183	168
Dhangar	69	10	—		—	79	69
Gavali	14	—	—		4	18	—
Vani	1	5	—		—	6	4
Pardeshi	—	1	5	3	14	23	75
Kachi	—	—	—		—	—	5
Lingayat	2	5	—		11	18	43
Others	—	4	10	1	14	29	—
Total Number	186	63	37	9	67	362	427
Per Cent	7.9	10.4	6.0	5.8	12.6	8.5	7.6
Village Artisans							
Sonar	1	4	16	1		22	58
Shimpi	15		16	4	9	44	100
Kasar	—		—	1		1	14
Sali, Vinkar	140	6	—			146	130
Tambat	—		5			5	19
Lohar	14		—			14	9
Sutar	1		—			1	38
Others	—	5	1			6	—
Total Number	171	15	38	6	9	239	368
Per Cent	7.3	2.6	6.1	3.7	1.8	5.6	6.6

233

APPENDIX B (continued)

Caste	Textile	Paper	Engine	Biscuit	Rubber	Total Factory	Poona Population
Village Servants							
Joshi	13				5	18	5
Gurav	14	6			4	24	7
Nhavi	14		5			19	46
Parit	1	11			9	21	27
Kumbhar	—	11				11	15
Koli, Bhoi	98	19		1	9	127	51
Ramoshi	1	14			5	20	16
Teli	43			1	2	46	16
Others	—	5				5	—
Total Number	184	66	5	2	34	291	183
Per Cent	7.8	10.9	0.8	1.7	6.5	6.8	3.3
Backward Castes							
Mahar	125	30	58	1	5	219	342
Chambhar	—	35	—	—	—	35	67
Mang	14	—	10	—	—	24	142
Bhangi	—	—	—	1	—	1	30
Vadar	14	5	—	—	—	19	40
Kaikadi	—	19	—	—	—	19	—
Others	55	47	6	2	51	161	81
Total Number	208	30	74	4	56	478	702
Per Cent	8.9	22.5	12.1	2.5	10.5	11.2	12.5
Other Regions							
Telegu	123	10	16	1	5	155 ⎫	143
Tamil	—	—	5		9	14 ⎬	
Kannadi	16	—	—			16	—
Gujarati	10	—	6			16	—
Marwari	—	1	—			1	30
Punjabi	9	—	—		5	14	17
Sindhi	—	—	—	1	1	2	80
Gurkha	—	—	—	3		3	—
Rajput, Thakur	69	10	5	3		87	36
Others	—	15	—	1	26	42	—
Total Number	227	36	32	9	46	350	392
Per Cent	9.7	5.9	5.3	5.6	8.6	8.2	7.0

APPENDIX B (concluded)

Caste	Textile	Paper	Engine	Biscuit	Rubber	Total Factory	Poona Population
her Religions							
Muslim	166	26	21	1	19	233	454
ʃain	—	—	—		—	—	126
Christian	27	5	39		15	86	226
Parsi	—	1	—		—	1	39
Jew	—	—	5		—	5	4
Buddhist	27	9	11		9	56	—
Sikh	—	5	—		4	9	22
Others	—	—	—		5	5	—
tal Number	220	46	76	1	52	395	871
r Cent	9.4	7.7	12.2	0.8	9.8	9.3	15.5
Response	—	—	—	—	3	3	—
RAND TOTAL	2342	603	614	159	531	4249	5279[a]

[a] Source of Poona table is detailed tabulation of caste and community provided by vani, which was then reclassified into the present categories; 322 or 5.8 percent of the ses in the Poona sample were in miscellaneous caste groups that could not be redivided ɔperly and they have been omitted.

APPENDIX C

Occupational Class	Textile	Paper	Engine	Biscuit	Rubber	All Factories
Clerks	—	—	52.0	5.6	43.5	20.9
Supervisors	13.1	10.5	13.6	—	15.4	11.8
P & M workers	19.0	20.7	34.0	38.8	53.9	26.3

MEAN NUMBER OF FAMILY MEMBERS IN HOUSEHOLD OF EACH
OCCUPATIONAL CLASS, BY FACTORY

Occupational Class	Textile	Paper	Engine	Biscuit	Rubber	All Factories
Clerks	6.1	6.1	5.8	4.6	5.8	5.9
Supervisors	5.3	6.1	5.5	5.2	5.2	5.5
P & M workers	4.5	5.3	5.9	4.5	4.5	5.1

PERCENTAGE OF SPOUSES EMPLOYED IN EACH OCCUPATIONAL
CLASS, BY FACTORY

Occupational Class	Textile	Paper	Engine	Biscuit	Rubber	All Factories
Clerks	22.2	—	—	—	7.7	9.7
Supervisors	1.4	5.9	5.3	—	—	2.7
P & M workers	5.5	22.7	—	6.7	4.3	7.0

MEAN NUMBERS OF NON-EARNERS PER EARNER IN FAMILY HOUSEHOLDS
OF CLERKS, SUPERVISORS, AND LABORERS, BY FACTORY

Occupational Class	Textile	Paper	Engine	Biscuit	Rubber	All Factories
Clerks	3.1	3.2	3.1	2.6	2.7	3.0
Supervisors	3.1	3.3	2.9	2.8	2.8	3.1
Laborers	2.7	2.7	2.7	2.1	2.1	2.6

APPENDIX C (concluded)

MONTHLY PER CAPITA INCOME, IN RUPEES, IN FAMILY HOUSEHOLDS
OF CLERKS, SUPERVISORS, AND LABORERS, BY FACTORY

Occupational Class	Textile	Paper	Engine	Biscuit	Rubber	All Factories
Clerks	37.2	29.0	52.6	45.0	41.1	41.1
Supervisors	42.1	33.7	79.5	51.7	58.8	46.7
P & M workers	28.5	26.5	31.3	30.4	31.6	29.1

APPENDIX D

PERCENTAGE OF MIGRANTS IN EACH OCCUPATIONAL CLASS, BY FACTORY

Occupational Class	Textile	Paper	Engine	Biscuit	Rubber	All Factories
Clerks	66.7	100.0	80.0	66.7	65.2	73.7
Supervisors	82.1	34.2	54.5	58.3	84.6	66.2
P & M workers	74.0	55.0	66.0	64.6	70.6	69.5

PERCENTAGE OF WORKERS FROM OTHER THAN MAHARASHTRA, IN EACH OCCUPATIONAL CLASS, BY FACTORY

Occupational Class	Textile	Paper	Engine	Biscuit	Rubber	All Factories
Clerks	57.1	—	25.0	23.1	16.7	31.9
Supervisors	75.4	40.0	41.1	50.0	41.7	58.6
P & M workers	39.1	28.4	28.1	47.8	68.8	40.0

PERCENTAGE OF WORKERS WITH A MOTHER TONGUE OTHER THAN MARATHI, IN EACH OCCUPATIONAL CLASS, BY FACTORY

Occupational Class	Textile	Paper	Engine	Biscuit	Rubber	All Factories
Clerks	44.4	20.0	8.0	—	—	20.8
Supervisors	11.9	15.8	18.2	8.3	30.8	15.2
P & M workers	22.2	23.4	16.5	20.8	32.4	22.8

APPENDIX E

On 26th November 1954, the Paper Kamgar Sabha, a registered trade union, addressed a letter to the management of the ———— Paper Mills Co., enclosing a charter of demands. As no agreement was possible between the parties, intervention of this office was sought. The membership record of the union shows that it has 450 workmen as members out of the total number of 585 employed by the Company. The dispute concerns all workmen employed in the factory excluding clerical staff. The dispute was taken in conciliation on ———————— and after some discussion the following settlement was arrived at:

TERMS OF SETTLEMENT

Demand

1. Wage Scale

Agreement

The wage Scale shall be in the following grades:

Grade A— Rs. 1-0-0/0-1-0/1-10-0
B— Rs. 1-4-0/0-1-0/2-0-0
C— Rs. 1-8-0/0-2-0/2-8-0
D— Rs. 1-10-0/0-2-6/3-0-6
E— Rs. 2-0-0/0-3-0/3-8-0
F— Rs. 3-0-0/0-4-0/5-0-0

The classification of the workmen in Grade A to F shall be as annexture A.
The following shall be the special grades:

1. Head Sweeper	Rs.	45-3-60
2. Cook	"	45-3-60
3. Mali	"	30-2-40
4. Despatch Peons	"	45-3-60
5. Watchman	"	37-3-52
6. Jamadars	"	45-4-65
7. Motor Drivers and Lorry Drivers	"	50-3-65-4-101
8. Motor Cleaners	"	35-3-50
9. Mucadams Male and Female	"	45-3-60
10. Cartmen	"	1-8-0/0-2-0/2-8-0 per day

It is further agreed that the cartmen will be paid Rs. 2/-per day as Cart allowance per pair of bullocks.

239

11. Weighers   Rs. 1-8-0/0-2/0/2-8-0
12. Turners   " 3-0-0/0-4-0/5-0-0
13. Sarangs   " 3-0-0/0-4-0/5-0-0

Wages for these special Grades shall be for the working days in the month.

14. Finishers:

The company shall prepare a new scale for finishers having relation to output before 31-3-1955 and send the same to the Sabha. Till that date, the present scale to continue. Agreement in respect of such scale when arrived at, shall be incorporated in a separate agreement and will be given effect to after the signing of such an agreement by the Sabha and by the management.

15. Bailers   Rs. 1-4-0/0-1-6/2-0-0
    The piece rate will be:
      Grade I -0-3-0/0-0-3/0-4-0 per bale
      Grade II-0-2-6/0-0-3/0-3-6 per bale

All increments in the aforesaid scales shall be given on the 1st of January of each year.
Additional Payments:

1. Chopper feeder coolies working in night shift—As. 2 per ton
2. Female carriers—As. 2 per ton
3. Female chopper feeder coolies—As. 2 per ton
4. Rag Boiler Attendants—As. 2 per boiler
5. Chopper Feeders shall be paid bonus at the rate of As. 6 per 4000 lbs. of rags chopped.
6. Weighers shall be paid a bonus of As. 4 per day.

Dearness Allowance   It is agreed between the parties that the workmen other than the members of the clerical and supervisory staff, shall be paid Dearness Allowance equivalent to 67½% of the amount of Dearness Allowance paid to the operatives in the textile Mills in Bombay City and calculated according to the method which prevailed till 30th November 1954.

Gratuity   It is agreed between the parties that the company shall pay to all its workmen till the introduction of Provident Fund Scheme under the

Employees Provident Fund Act, 1952 or of a Scheme with a rate of contributions as provided for under the said act, gratuity on the following scale:

1. On the death of the employee while in service of the company or on his becoming physically or mentally incapable of further service—half month's basic salary or wages for each year of continuous service to be paid to the disabled employee or if he had died, to his heirs or legal representatives or assigns.

2. On Voluntary retirement or resignation of an employee after 15 years continuous service —half month's basic salary or wages for each year of continuous service.

3. On termination of service by the company— half month's basic salary or wages for each year of completed service.

The following conditions shall govern the grant of gratuity:—

a) Gratuity shall not be payable to a workman dismissed for misconduct.

b) Salary or wages for the purpose of gratuity shall be the last salary or wages exclusive of Dearness Allowance drawn at the date of death, disability, retirement, resignation or termination as the case may be.

In case of workers working on piece rates, wage shall mean the average basic earnings per day calculated on the basis of his total basic earnings during the preceding three months.

c) The scheme of gratuity shall apply to all permanent workmen and also to those who have ceased to be the workmen of the company by reason of death, disability, retirement, resignation or termination of services since 8th January 1952.

d) No permanent worker shall be entitled to gratuity in respect of his service period as and from 1st November 1952 i.e., as and from the date on which Provident Fund Scheme under the Employees' Provident Fund Act 1952 has been brought into force in respect of the employees of the Mill.

e) Permanent worker who is played out or retrenched and who receives compensation under the I.D. Amendment Act 1954, shall not be entitled for the benefit of Gratuity under the aforesaid scheme. The following 9 workmen who are at present getting pension stated against their names shall continue to get such monthly pension with dearness allowance but they shall not be entitled for any other benefits under this agreement.

	Pension	Addition to Pension	Amount
1. S.S.	12-0-0	30% D.A.	3-9-6
2. K.K.	7-0-0	do	2-1-6
3. M.R.	4-0-0	do	1-3-3
4. C.R.	7-0-0	do	2-1-6
5. G.M.	5-0-0	do	1-8-0
6. G.A.	7-0-0	do	2-1-6
7. A.L.	7-0-0	do	2-1-6
8. R.M.	7-0-0	do	2-1-6
9. G.P.	6-8-0	do	1-15-6

Leave Facilities

Casual Leave: It is agreed that the workmen will be entitled to 7 days casual leave in the year subject to the following terms and conditions:

1. Casual leave shall be allowed only for emergent and unforeseen circumstances and shall be subject to the exigencies of work in the factory.

2. Not more than 3 days casual leave shall be taken at a time and the leave shall not be allowed to be added to weekly off or holiday.
Privilege Leave: The company shall grant 20 days sick leave with 10 days full pay and dearness allowance for each year with a right to accumulate the same for two consecutive years. Sick leave shall be granted on production of a certificate from a registered Medical Practitioner or Mill Doctor.

Festival Holidays

The Company shall give to its employees the following four paid holidays:

(1) 26th January (2) 15th August
(3) Diwali and (4) Mundwha Village Urus.

Uniforms

a) Uniforms as mentioned in clause (b) below shall be given to the following workers:—

242

1. Watchmen and Jamadar, 2. Office Boys,
3. Oilmen, 4. Creche Nurses,
5. Firemen, 6. Chopper Feeders,
7. Drivers.

b) For the female workmen the uniforms shall be two sarees and two polkas per year. For motor drivers, office boys, despatch peons, watchmen and Jamadars the uniforms shall consist of a pair of long pants and coats, and all the rest of the male workmen shall be provided with a pair shorts and shirts.

The company shall provide uniforms in January of each year.

Substitutes

The company's present practice of paying 50 per cent of the difference between the salary of the workman who officiates and the workmen for whom he is officiating shall be continued. In case where the salary of the officiating workman in the lower grade is higher than the grade for whom he officiates, then the officiating workmen shall get one increment over his own higher salary.

Contract Labour

The company shall have the right to employ contract labour for work of emergent and casual nature, but not for the normal work of the Mills.

Social Amenities

Injections and patent medicines will not be provided by the company but if any employee gets the prescribed injections the Company's Doctor will administer them free of charge. Otherwise the company will provide medical treatment by way of medicines to the workmen.

It is further agreed that parties to the agreement can re-open any of the above clauses after one year from the date this settlement comes into effect by giving notice of termination to the particular clause only and terminating of the whole of the settlement shall not be necessary.

This settlement shall come into effect from 30th November 1954.

INDEX

acquiescence effect, 199

age of workers, compared with Poona population, 24-26; differences among factories, 44-45; commitment, 87; of temporary workers, 102; occupational class, 145-47; aspiration level, 188; favorableness to company, 214

Ahmedabad Textile Industry Research Association, 118

Ambedkar, B. R., 34

Apte, D. P., 8

aspiration levels, 16-17, 168-69, 182-93, 221-22

badli system, *see* temporary workers

Bass, Bernard M., 199n

Blumer, Herbert, 17n

Brown, W. Norman, 80n

caste, 30-35; by factory, 49-50; and occupational category, 147, 153-62; vs. education, vi-vii, 162-65; workers' perceptions of, 166-68; and aspirations, 188; detailed tables, 232-34

Choudry, Kamla, 118-19

commitment, workers', 5, 6, 8, 79-95; employers', 94-104

complement of workers, 94-95, 239-43

dearness allowances (DA), 109-10, 115-16

dependency load, vi, 40-43, 142-43, 143. *See also* families of workers

education, compared with Poona population, 28-29; differences among factories, 45-48; use of employment exchanges, 75; commitment, 87; occupational

category, 147, 149-52; vs. caste, 162-65; aspiration level, 168-70, 188

employment exchanges, 71-75

English, knowledge of, 26-28, 49, 30, 147-49

experience, previous occupational, 59-66; use of employment exchanges, 87; wages, 170; aspiration level, 188

families of workers, of women employees, 24; compared with Poona population, 38-43; differences among factories, 52-56; use in hiring, 77-79; commitment, 87; relations with factory, 105-06; occupational rank, 142-43; detailed tables, 236-37. *See also* dependency load

favorableness to the company, vii, 193-214

Feldman, Arnold S., *see* Moore, Wilbert

fringe benefits, 94, 109-10, 239-43

Gadgil, D. R., v-viii

Gemeinschaft and *Gesellschaft*, 15, 16-17, 224

Goode, William J., 39n

Goodman, L. S., 211n

government and labor relations, 92, 94, 97, 114, 239-43

Guttman scale, 208-11

Hauser, Philip M., 79n

Hindi, knowledge of, 26-28, 49

hiring practices, 70-79, 93

Hoselitz, Bert F., 80n

Hoyt, C. J., 210n

industrialization and traditional society, stages of industrialization, v, 9-10; parallels, vii, 91-